NEW ENGLAND
CITIZEN SOLDIERS
of the REVOLUTIONARY WAR

NEW ENGLAND CITIZEN SOLDIERS
of the REVOLUTIONARY WAR

° *Minutemen & Mariners* °

with all good
wishes —

ROBERT A. GEAKE

THE
History
PRESS

Published by The History Press
Charleston, SC
www.historypress.com

First published 2019

Manufactured in the United States

ISBN 9781467142601

Library of Congress Control Number: 2019945081

CONTENTS

PREFACE

In John Miller's influential work *Origins of the American Revolution*, we find the opinion that the English in waging war on North America "generally overlooked what proved to be one of America's most serious weaknesses during the War of Independence: the conviction that the militia were the guardians of liberty and that a regular standing army was its eternal enemy."

This belief was indeed widespread, not limited to rural areas, where there was no debate whatsoever, but also in the urban centers of America. The motto beneath the banner of Boston's *Continental Weekly and Adviser* in 1778 read, "The Entire Propriety of Every State Depends Upon the Discipline of its Armies." The quote, attributed to the king of Prussia, may well have been intended to mean the "nation state," but Americans thought differently, and even into the war that united those separate "armies" into one cause, the concerns of each state were sometimes placed above any notion of allegiance to the idea of "one nation."

The contributions of the militia to the American Revolution are irrefutable but often misunderstood—from the mythology grown from the minutemen to the mistrust and grumbling from Washington and other officers as they tried to make these bands of independent men conform to the standards of a standing army to the guerrilla tactics that unnerved the enemy and underscored the American victory.

Their influence on the public imagining of the war would ensure that independent militias would remain the "citizen soldiers" of their communities. The young men who enlisted to serve in the local militia were often taking an opportunity to gain status in their communities, as this book will show.

For many historians and readers of military history, there is a distinct difference between the "regulars," or enlisted men of the Continental army, and the militia, composed of men who served part time in local companies. These men were mostly entrusted with protecting their communities and aiding with supplies during the war but were also frequently called on to march to a neighboring colony/state to shore up defenses there—or march into battle when Washington assembled troops for a major campaign.

The first Continental army assembled began with conscripts from those same local militias—the officers first and then those men who passed the age and physical requirements to serve. It is important to note again that the states/colonies had no standing army, and the majority of Americans held the view that a standing army was anathema to democracy. Of the many written opinions on the issue from that time, perhaps Samuel Adams in writing to his friend James Warren expressed their reasons most succinctly:

> [A] *standing army, however necessary it may be at some times, is always dangerous to the liberties of the people. Soldiers are apt to consider themselves as a body distinct from the rest of the citizens. They have their arms always in their hands. Their rules and their discipline is severe. They soon become attached to their officers and disposed to yield implicit obedience to their commands. Such a power should be watched with a jealous eye.*[1]

The Articles of Confederation, the precursor to our Constitution, authorized Congress only to assemble a navy and only referenced those "land forces" that would be gathered by the states from their militia and other enlisted citizens.

Many of those who enlisted in the Continental army served their nine-month terms and returned home, sometimes keeping active in local defense and other times reenlisting in the army after several months absent. Militiamen drilled on a regular basis and were called "on alarm" to serve for times that varied from a week to several months.

The very idea of Congress holding any military power brought a flurry of proposals to limit any such authority from representatives of Massachusetts, Pennsylvania, New Jersey and Connecticut. While Washington had envisioned the army and militia as having a "separate but mutually supportive role to play" in the war effort, those hopes became only partially realized. When the general requested a draft in December 1776, he was rebuffed, and the matter of enlistments was passed along to the states/colonies.

While Congress approved Washington's recommendations as to the size and organization of the state militias, each state/colony struggled to fulfill its quota during the war, and often men served both at home and "abroad." In so doing, the lines between those who served in state militias and the Continental army continued to overlap and sometimes blurred the lines between identification as a "regular" or "militia."

As historian Don Higginbotham described, "Fear of American militarism, of a real standing army, increased with the lengthening of the war: Congress soon found it incumbent to re-enlist men for three years, or the duration of the war…manpower shortages resulted in the Continental Army's bearing a growing resemblance to classic European armies. Criminals, British deserters, servants, drifters and the like were taken into service as Congress scraped the bottom of the barrel of human resources."[2]

Regardless of their origin (enlisted or drafted), those who served in militia or as privateers were all citizen soldiers who served and contributed, no matter whether at home or far from their farms and families, and played their part in winning the American War of Independence.

ACKNOWLEDGEMENTS

My sincere thanks to the librarians at the Rhode Island Historical Society's Robinson Research Center, particularly Jennifer Galpern and Michelle Chiles, who assisted me in navigating the large collection of Revolutionary War papers in the collections.

I would also like to acknowledge information gathered from Historic New England, the Warwick Historical Society, the Massachusetts Historical Society, the John Carter Brown and John Hay Libraries at Brown University and the archives of the Cocumscussoc Association and the James Mitchell Varnum Museum.

Thanks must also be given to Norman Desmarais, professor emeritus of Providence College; Patrick Donovan, curator of the Varnum Museum; David Matthew Proccacini, director of the Nathanael Greene Homestead; Brian Mack, director of the Fort Plain Museum; historian James F. Morrison; Mike Kinsella of The History Press, as well as my editor, Ryan Finn; and to Christian McBurney, who has served as a mentor in my ventures into writing of the Revolutionary War.

This book is dedicated to Captain John Billings, John Billings Jr., Benjamin Billings, Solomon Billings and Timothy Batchelder, known ancestors who served in the American Revolution, and in memory of my beloved uncle Malcolm Kenney (1925–2008), B-52 pilot for the U.S. Army Air Corps during the Second World War, recipient of the Distinguished Flying Cross and the Air Medal with cluster.

Part I

AN ARMY OF CITIZEN SOLDIERS

Chapter 1

RAISING A MILITIA FOR THE COMMON DEFENSE

Early militia in British North America were formed on the model of the citizen soldier—that is, those male citizens of the community who were fit for service would muster as a common militia on a regular basis, in preparedness for the defense of the settlement or town.

A militia unit, as with any organization, also became what we today would call a social network. From early on in colonial America, young men who enlisted to serve in local militia were often taking an opportunity to gain status in their communities. Historian J.L. Bell noted that "those who committed themselves to training could rise up in the ranks of militia's, often a stepladder to success in their own communities…once a man received the rank of Captain or higher, he retains that title throughout his life as a mark of respect."[3]

The Massachusetts Bay Colony received its charter on March 4, 1629, and the following month, the governing body issued its first General Letter of Instruction, appointing John Endicott governor of the Plantation at Naumkcac, later named the village of Salem.

Among his first actions taken as governor was to order the formation of a militia. The first such formation in North America was in Virginia as early as 1607. The militia of Massachusetts would be responsible for protecting a wide tract of land, effectively from Salem north and west into present-day New Hampshire.

Endicott was well aware from the start that he had to present his militia as a disciplined and orderly unit and commissioned from Great Britain

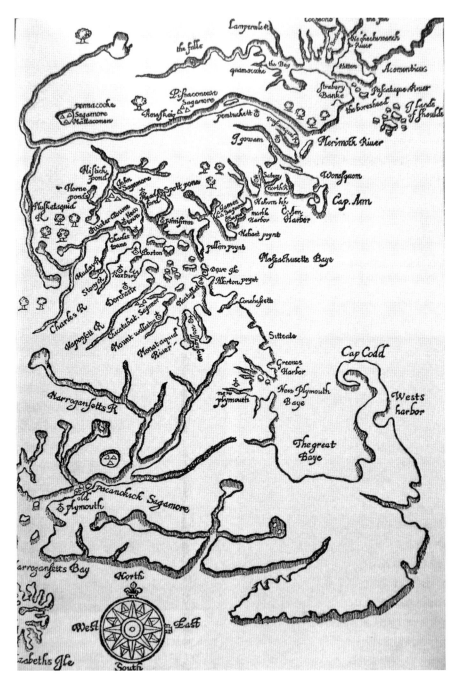

Early map of New England as it appeared in William Wood's *New England's Prospect. Courtesy of the John Carter Brown Library at Brown University.*

"100 green coats bound with red tape"—a duplicate of the "camouflage" uniforms used in Ireland during that period.

The weapons sent for the use of the militia included eight cannons for use at a defensive fortification and one hundred firearms—"80 flintlocks, 10 long fowling pieces, 10 large caliber matchlocks."[4] One hundred swords were also dispatched, as were eighty-three pole arms, sixty pikes and twenty half-pikes. The men also received sixty corsets of body armor.

On August 25, 1630, the General Court established requirements for universal military service that compelled all adult males (except ministers and magistrates) to possess arms. Towns were required to furnish arms for those who could not afford them, and a standard load of ammunition was also set for each town. Two military veterans, Captains Daniel Patrick and John Underhill, were chosen to train the colony's militia.

On April 12, 1631, the General Court issued a directive that "every captain(s) shall traine his companie on Saterday in everie weeke." By November 1632, the training day had been cut back to once a month, and eventually the months of July and August were excluded to allow farms to be tended. However, captains still retained the right to require additional training, up to three days a week, for men who had not proved proficient in arms.

Some companies, such as the first Salem militia, were split between several towns initially, with a goal of one hundred men per company. This would lead to the first split-training by Captain John Underhill's company, which included men from "Boston, Roxbury, Charlestown, Mystick, and New Town."[5]

By the 1760s, when political tensions began to seriously rise, the Boston Train Artillery regularly exercised and recruited new members. Such exercises also sent the message back to Great Britain that "[w]e colonists can defend ourselves, so there is no need for a standing army in America or for higher taxes to pay for that army."[6]

The Massachusetts militia enforced their loyalty to the people of the colony when some thirty-seven companies marched on the town of Worcester to prevent the Court of Common Pleas and the Court of General Sessions from convening for the first time under the British-sanctioned Massachusetts Government Act, which overturned democratic safeguards that had been granted the colony since 1691.[7]

The closure had been in the planning since July 4, 1774, when the American Political Society, whose members were also in the local militia, determined to provide each of its members with flints and gunpowder.

Committees of Correspondence from twenty-two towns in Worcester County also convened to discuss "those most alarming acts of parliament, respecting our constitution."

When the citizens of Berkshire County forced the closure of the courts, the die was cast. The Worcester County Committee of Correspondence met again on August 30 and urged a great turnout and protest when the court again convened. In that call for the citizenry to turn out, the delegates wrote to town officials, urging that they send their militia to monitor the crowds under the strictest orders to act as soldiers and keep the mob from becoming unruly.

On September 2, militia began to muster for the march, and a rumor swirled that the British had set Boston ablaze. The misinformation may have contributed to the number of men who mustered, for some 4,622 militiamen descended on Worcester four days later. More rumors had circulated that Governor Thomas Gage would send troops to protect the courts and confront the militia.

Indeed, Gage had planned to do just that, but the unrest being so widespread "and not confined to any particular spot," sending troops to quell each disturbance in the towns would mean sending "small Detachments and tempt Numbers to fall upon them."[8] Word came of Gage's decision before the "body of the people" reached Worcester, and word was sent out by the American Political Society that guns were no longer a necessity, though by one account, about one thousand militiamen brought their arms to the courthouse. Violence had been avoided in this instance, although it was a prelude of actions and affairs to come in Massachusetts.

The separate colonies of Connecticut and New Haven merged to form what became the colony of Connecticut in May 1665. Those separate colonies had similar rules for militia service and training. A reprint of the 1702 Acts and Laws allowed that "all men between sixteen and sixty, except magistrates, justices of the peace, the secretary, church officers, allowed physicians, surgeons, school masters, representatives or deputies… constant herdsmen, mariners, sheriffs, constables, constant ferrymen, lame persons, indians, and negroes were required to participate in regular training exercises and to bear arms."[9]

As the colony's population expanded, so did the regiments protecting new counties, and by 1739, the Assembly had created regimental staff to oversee the increase in militia companies. There were thirteen regiments covering the colony in 1739, and little would change for the next thirty years, in which time three new regiments—the Fourteenth, Fifteenth and Sixteenth—were added.

In May 1774, the Assembly added two more, commanded by Colonels Oliver Walcott and Jonathan Pettibone.[10]

Connecticut recruited its first volunteers for service at Boston in the spring of 1775. On April 21, 1775, word reached New Haven at noon of the British march on Lexington. One Yale student wrote that once the news had reached campus, it was impossible "to attend to our studies with any profit."

Young lieutenant Martin Sylvanius would write of the march to Boston and the battle there in his journal, which he began on June 7, 1775, with this entry: "Wensday the Company under Colo George Pikins Rais by order of the general assembly for the Defence of the Colony of Conecut & Consisting of one hundred men…Marched on our jorney to Boston."

During the following week, the men would march through the towns of Ashford, Woodstock, Sutton, Westbury, Framingham and Brookline. On Wednesday, June 14, the men witnessed the arrival of some three thousand regulars. The following day, the lieutenant wrote, "The Regulars are this Day Exercising their horses which is supposed they intend to Risk a battle soon." His company was assigned to dig trenches on Bunker Hill. On the day following:

> *Our men were discovered in the morning & fired on from the ships in the harber and killd one man belonging to* [Colonel] *Putnam. This morning we moved in one house Belonging to hulton a torry now in Boston we are 2 miles from Roxbery meting house this Day the Cannon fird all Day on Charls Town & on Roxbery about 6 o'clock Charlstown took fire & about 2 or 3 thousans regelers marcht to our intrench-ments which formed in Devittions & were all most cut of for 3 times & their* [fought] *our works by the Loss of 1500 killd & wounded & on our side not 200 lost.*[11]

Most of these men would be adopted into the Continental army, and while some officers were taken from local militia units, their service lasted only into early December. The following spring, eight new Continental regiments were formed, stripping the best men and officers from local militia, as well as the boys and men of the town who volunteered. The loss of leadership within local militia would cause much turmoil.[12]

By the summer of 1776, Connecticut had twenty-five militia regiments of foot and five militia regiments of light horse. In December 1776, the Assembly formed the regiments into six militia brigades, each commanded by a brigadier general. Historian John K. Robertson explained, "This allowed the Council of Safety to deal with six men instead of thirty."[13]

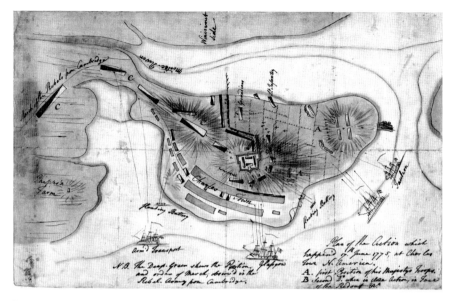

Map of Charlestown, Massachusetts. *From Carrington's* Battles of the American Revolution.

The Assembly also instituted an "alarm list" separate from the muster rolls of militia and volunteers. The list effectively obliged those men who had not passed muster in their respective communities to remain prepared, provide themselves with arms and to serve if needed, on any alarm.

In March 1680, the king of England authorized New Hampshire's colonial president, John Cutt, to "give commissions to persons who shall be best qualified for regulating and discipline of the militia." Cutt appointed Major Richard Waldron of Dover as the first commander of the militia.

As the New Hampshire territory was then part of the Massachusetts Bay Colony, the men of this early militia were part of the provincial forces that aided British regulars in the siege of the French outpost of Port Royal in 1710.

The territory was granted its independence from Massachusetts in 1740. The militia were next dispatched when Provincial Governor Benning Wentworth aligned with the Massachusetts Bay Colony under Governor William Shirley in seeking support from the neighboring colonies in an attack on the French fortress at Louisburg in 1745. New Hampshire would contribute 450 men to the siege, which eventually captured the fortress at what is now Cape Breton.

The French and Indian War (1754–63) saw the colony contribute some five thousand troops who served in six different campaigns. Major

Robert Rogers led a regiment that included John Stark, who would later become brigadier general of the state militia and a general during the Revolutionary War.

In 1755, the colony mustered a regiment of three companies under command of Joseph Blanchard. The men of the company varied in age from young to old. Most were farmers or farmhands and so dressed in homespun shirts and breeches, with slouch wool hats pulled over their brows. They carried their own muskets or hunting rifles, with a knife or hatchet slung from their belts.

Caricature of an American militia meeting. *From* Gentlemen's Magazine, *London, 1775.*

In a show of force, the New Hampshire Provincial Congress ordered Blanchard to parade the troops to the Connecticut River, along a trail blazed by Rogers and Stark two years earlier. It was during that expedition that Stark had been taken prisoner by the indigenous tribe of the region for constructing a road through what they told the settlers was sacred land.

Blanchard's men reached the Connecticut River without incident, but then, rather than heading through the uncharted wilderness of Vermont, as had originally been planned, they were ordered to march south along the river's eastern bank to Fort Number Four. The next day, they crossed the river to Fort Drummond and from there on to Albany and war.

As tensions with Great Britain increased, the state and local militia were reactivated. John Stark commanded the New Hampshire militia, and between 1774 and 1777, the state contributed men to the war effort from thirteen separate militias formed in communities from Cornish to Walpole and from Plymouth to Rockingham County. Captain Nathan Hale was among the first to command a company of what were now being called minutemen. Colonel John Moulton's regiment was called to the alarm to guard the New Hampshire coastline in April 1775, after the British had burned the town of Falmouth, now Portland, Maine, in what was then still part of the Massachusetts Bay Colony.

Neighboring Vermont was a different story. Besieged by land claims from New York and New Hampshire, the years before the call for the colonies to be "united or die" had been filled with tension and conflict. In March 1775, the hostilities between the encroaching New Yorkers and Vermont settlers erupted in violence, with the resultant deaths of two local men. In the wake of what was called the "Westminster Massacre," the colony raised an independent army to protect its borders and appointed Ethan Allen as commander of what would become known as the Green Mountain Boys.

Despite these tensions, Allen mustered the men to answer the alarm in the spring of 1775, and regiments from the Green Mountain Boys subsequently took part in the capture of Fort Ticonderoga, as well as several other key battles early in the war.

As with the other colonies, men stayed behind for duty, whether mustering for preparedness, contributing to the supply chain for troops in a campaign or being called to battle. A pay roll from that year of 1775 shows that a company of minutemen under Captain Thomas Johnson held fifty-one men, including junior officers, who served anywhere from two days to thirty. Captain Thomas Lee's independent company of rangers held just thirty-seven men, from towns ranging from Rutland to Harwick, towns around Bennington County whose men would be thrust into battle relatively late in the war.[14]

Some had to wait years for compensation. A document from 1786 authorized payment to Captain Oliver Potter and his men who served in Seth Warner's regiment in the expedition to Canada. Officers were rewarded with cash for having enlisted the men who marched in Benedict Arnold's campaign, but those men who marched mainly received just under three and a half pounds, along with a gun and a blanket.

The colony of Providence Plantations, now known as Rhode Island, had established a small Trainee Band in the town of Portsmouth as early as 1638, proclaiming that all free men of the community were "subject to call and expected to perform certain military duties for the protection of the people." Neighboring towns held similar laws. Newport had a troop of horse in 1667, led by Captain Peleg Sandford, as well as a "Train Band upon the island." The troops muster roll included Governor William Brenton, who provided his own horse and furniture (a saddle) with his service.[15]

For many years, the colony commissioned a general sergeant, later to be captain in chief, of the colony military force. In 1673, the Assembly also sanction the procuring of men in Newport and Portsmouth "for the Manageing of Boats to be employed in the Waters of this Bay, for the Colony's Defense."

But being a predominantly Quaker colony, a larger militia was effectively resisted in the Assembly until the violence that visited the town from King's County to Providence during King Philip's War.[16]

Looking out toward Gaspee Point from the shores of Narragansett Bay. *Photo by the author.*

In 1687, a letter from Governor William Hopkins was sent to Colonel John Fitz Winthrop with instructions and a list of "Solders belonging to your Company of Malisha." In May 1689, Major Roger Goulding was appointed commander of Militia of the Islands, with John Greene of Warwick continuing his role as commander of the Militia on the Main.[17]

Records show that in February 1714, the Militia of the Islands had added companies from Shoreham and Jamestown, with the Militia of the Main now expanding to contain companies from Providence, Warwick, Westerly, Kingston and Greenwich. Troops of horse were added to the Providence company and later as a full unit of the Militia on the Main. In 1723, a company from South Kingstown was added, with the Kingston Regiment becoming a North Kingstown company. By 1730, companies in Smithfield, Scituate and Gloucester had been added to the militia.

The colony would subsequently create a state militia in 1741, under which these individual militias would be conscripted in times of crises. These would include the provision of troops in Queen Anne's War, King George's War and the French and Indian War before the American Revolution.

Rhode Island was the smallest colony, barely a speck on the map of British cartographers but for Newport, an international seaport for both trade and slavery. Such was its importance that it was, after Boston and New York, the first city seized by the British on the Atlantic coast.

Rhode Islanders had responded to British intimidation of the colonies with the famous HMS *Gaspee* incident, during which a band of volunteers burned a British patrol schooner to the waterline after it had run aground. In the wake of the Boston Port Bill in June 1774, the citizens of the town of East Greenwich responded by collecting subscriptions and money to help the Bostonians.

There were tensions in the town despite this support, and on September 13, 1774, a riot stirred by Loyalists to the Crown had formed as a mob and threatened to burn the town. Companies of light infantry and cadets had to be called from Providence to quell the disturbance.[18]

Eleven days later, "with a sense of shameful neglect of military exercise," some forty-nine men of the town met at the William Arnold Tavern on Main Street and entered into a compact to form a "military independent company." Among the signers were two men who would become the most prominent of the Rhode Islanders who entered the Continental army: attorney James Mitchell Varnum and forge owner Nathanael Greene. This

Left: Portrait of General James Mitchell Varnum. *Courtesy of Brown University Collections.*

Right: Lithograph of General Nathanael Greene. *Courtesy of the Warwick Historical Society.*

militia unit, perhaps of all the others that formed in the state, came about by a turn of history and from the most unlikely of leaders.

Nathanael Greene was born into an old Rhode Island Quaker family, descendants of James Greene, who settled the area in 1680. His father, for whom he was named, was a leader at the local meetinghouse and a businessman as well, continuing the family tradition of farming and shipping goods along the Atlantic coast. He also established a forge on the Pawtuxet River in Coventry. The young Greene grew up working his father's expansive and rock-cropped farm at Potowamut.

By the time he was twenty-eight, Greene was placed in charge of the forge. His father had built a fine Federal-style house for him there.

The young Greene was a self-made man in every sense of meaning the phrase holds. Although his Quaker family was well-to-do, their humble life in faith also meant a sparse education for the children of the family. Nathanael would undertake the task of earning his own education, with

Nathanael Greene Homestead, Coventry, Rhode Island. *Photo by the author.*

assistance and support from a number of friends and acquaintances outside the Quaker community.

One such person was the minister Ezra Stiles, one of the prime intellectuals of his age, who was then minister of the Second Congregational Church in Newport. Stiles advised and encouraged the young Greene in his studies and wrote recommendations to others for assistance with the young man's education. Students who became acquainted with Greene, namely William Gill from Yale and Lindley Murray, who studied law, also encouraged Greene, lent books to the proficient reader and introduced him to the social graces he needed to acquire to become a gentleman. Later, David Howell, a tutor at the College of Rhode Island, would also be an intellectual benefactor of great service to Greene.

Nathanael Greene's standing in the local community grew with the success of the forge, as well as from the reputation he had earned as a manager. In 1770, Greene was selected to represent the town in the Rhode Island General Assembly. It was during his term there that a turn of history would propel him into the revolutionary upheaval that was to come.

Although Greene was away from Potowomut visiting friends on the night of June 9, 1772, he surely relished the actions taken against the British revenue schooner *Gaspee* as it lay aground on the long sandbar off Namquid Point, just above the entrance to the Providence River. The *Gaspee* had hounded ships carrying goods from Warwick to Newport for several weeks, and the debate continues today as to whether the *Hannah*, a vessel that was owned by the Greene family, lured the ship to the sandbar or whether, as is more likely, a poor knowledge of the bay led to the ship running aground.

In the months that followed, Greene took it upon himself to drill with the Plainfield militia, and in 1773, facing a party of elders from the meetinghouse, he was read out of the Quaker meeting for participating in military exercises. This did not deter his study of military strategy or of what he perceived to be his impending duty.

After the compact to form a military company was signed in September 1774, Nathanael Greene and James Mitchell Varnum successfully petitioned the General Assembly of Rhode Island on October 29 to grant an Act of Incorporation, allowing them "and those who should be joined unto them" the formation of "an Independent Company by the name of the Kentish Guards."

They met openly at Arnold's tavern, distinguished by a wooden sign depicting a bunch of grapes that hung above the door in the center of town. The recruits trained on the nearby common, the far-flung fields of Potowomut and perhaps even the grounds above the forge on the Pawtuxet River.

The men had chosen Varnum as their commander despite his protestations that Nathanael Greene was more suited to the role. But reputedly because of a limp in Greene's gait due to a childhood accident, the men felt that Varnum would at least keep them in rhythm on the march. Greene, of course, would later become second in command to Washington in the Continental army. Varnum would also become a general in the Continental army before returning to head the local state militia.

Varnum's muster roll by January 1775 contained sixty-five enlistees, including young men from some of the most prominent families in the county, including Christopher Greene of Potowomet;[19] Jonathan Fry, the son of Benjamin; and Wanton Casey, son of the wealthy merchant Silas Casey, whose family farm expanded on the hillside above the western passage of Narragansett Bay.[20] The roll also includes Oliver Gardiner; Henry Jones, who may have been the oldest enlistee at sixty-three; and William Waterman.[21] Jonathan Greene (of Richard)[22] may have been a slave of the Greene family as well.

In fact, this small, independent company would contribute Varnum, General Nathanael Greene, Colonel Christopher Greene and various other lieutenant colonels, majors, captains and lieutenants to the Continental army.

The militia of the neighboring village of Pawtuxet would obtain their charter as the Pawtuxet Rangers on October 29, 1774. Their captain was Samuel Aborn, a sea captain who had used his sloop, *Sally*, to transport cannons and ammunition from the HMS *Gaspee* to be hidden in Pawtuxet. Aborn was also the host at the popular Golden Ball Inn at the western edge of the village on Post Road. Among other notable members of the Rangers were Captain Benjamin Arnold, Rhodes Arnold and Stephen Greene. According to the late Rhode Island historian Horace Belcher, "at least half of the membership bore the family names Aborn, Arnold, Rhodes, and Smith."

Historian William J. Staples wrote in his *Annals of the City of Providence*:

> *Providence at this juncture was not behind other places in making warlike preparations. It does not appear that any companies of minutemen were organized here. Their place was supplied by the Independent companies—so called—These consisted of volunteers from the militia, incorporated by the General Assembly and possessing certain privileges, among the most important of which was, that of choosing their own officers, subject only to approval*

by the Governor.…They were not attached to any particular regiments of the militia, nor subject to their general or regimental officers; but they received their orders immediately from the Governor, as Captain General.

In June 1774, the General Assembly named the body the Cadet Company and assigned a colonel to take command. In the same session, the Assembly ordered the formation of a light infantry company. By October, a grenadier company had been chartered and, at the close of the year, saw the organizing of the Providence Fusiliers as well as an artillery company.

Militias continued to spring like crocuses across the landscape of North America in the spring of 1775, and enlistments and formations of militia would continue to grow into the following year. Rhode Island was no exception.

As early as January 1775, Stephen Jenckes of North Providence had supplied several of the independent companies in Providence with muskets of his own manufacture.[23] On February 18, 1775, the *Providence Gazette* reported, "Not a day passes, Sundays excepted, but some of the companies are under arms; so well convinced are the people, that the complexion of the times renders a knowledge of the military art indispensably necessary."

News of the shots fired at Lexington and Concord would reach Rhode Island and the widow Zerviah Chapman at her daughter's home in Warwick, which she helped run as an inn. On April 22, 1775, Chapman recorded, "We had ye doleful news of ye fight between ye Regulars and Americans."[24]

That same day, the General Assembly enacted the charter of the United Companies of the Train of Artillery. The UTA was composed of the two companies, previously formed, the Fusiliers of Providence and the Artillery Company of Providence. The UTA's commander during the war was Colonel David Tillinghast of Newport. The UTA would join with Washington's forces in the Siege of Boston, being one of four in the army's combined artillery under command of Henry Knox. Their sixteen cannons contributed to the barrage from Dorchester Heights in the final stages of the siege in March 1776.

On the first Monday of April 1775, a general muster of the militia of the colony took place, on which occasion there were about two thousand men under arms in the county of Providence, besides the troop of horse.

Communities such as Providence had to constantly assess their preparedness for defense of the town. One Martin Seamans was charged with "making an examination into the state of the inhabitants on the East Side of the River with respect to Firearms, Bayonets, and Cartouche Boxes…and make return of the foregoing as a list of all who are supplied with the same as well as those who

Above: Detail from the charter for the Rhode Island Train of Artillery, 1776. *Courtesy of the James Mitchell Varnum Museum.*

Right: Illustration of the alarm beacon erected by the Providence River. *From Staple's* Annals of the City of Providence.

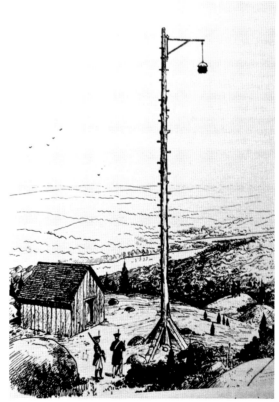

are not supplied—who by Law are obliged to be supplied with the same."[25] Conducted between February 6 and February 9, 1776, the document is one example of what was a widespread shortage of firepower against the British empire. Summarized here, Seamans found:

East Side of the River
Men…419
Guns…305
_____
Men more than guns…114

West Side of the River
Men…307
Guns…192
_____
Men more than guns…115

Total men: 726
Total guns: 297
Total men more than guns: 229

Most men received a gun apiece; others, however, namely prominent men in the community, received more. Merchant John Brown received three guns and his brother, Nicholas, four—presumably to arm their employees. Nicholas Cooke, who would serve part of the conflict as governor of the state, received six guns. Samuel Dunn Jr. and John Jenckes received five guns each. Charles Keen, Samuel Nightingale and Nuhemiah Power received four guns each. Seamans also found eight men "[l]ately moved into town that have no Arms."

Most of the arms, of course, were not in private homes but secluded at an ammunition post—sometimes a separate powder building was established. At other times, guns and ammunition were hidden at a safe location, a church being used in one Rhode Island town.

In Warwick, the widow Chapman's grandson, Lemuel Arnold (1759–1779), enlisted in the local militia before he reached the age of seventeen. His grandmother recorded on January 11, 1776, "Lem called away to Warwick Neck," the location of the largest of the fortifications that the town had built along its shoreline with Narragansett Bay. The following day, "Lem came home…called again in ye eve/man of war fired [on] Prudence Island."

The young man went to training on February 5 and then to Anthony Aborn's tavern in Pawtuxet, as well as to visit Caleb Battey, a neighbor of Aborn's who seems to have held religious services in his home that were often attended by his mother and grandmother. The young man's enlisting certainly would have gone against his father Simeon Arnold's wishes, for he was a devout Quaker, although it is clear the family held varying religious views. Such was the case for many of the young men of New England who eagerly enlisted at the outset of the war.

The town council moved its records to the "Fulling Mill" for safekeeping after the attack and also took an assessment of the firearms in the community. On February 12, 1776, during a meeting at the Fulling Mill, the council "resolved and voted that twenty-five arms well equipped with bayonets [and] cartridge boxes to be immediately purchased at the expense of the town." The council directed James Arnold, Colonel John Waterman and Colonel Samuel Aborn to purchase the weapons as soon as possible.[26]

The Pawtuxet Rangers had enough men for two divisions by April 1777. Oliver Arnold commanded the first division, with Sylvester Rhodes as junior officer. The division included three sergeants and seventeen privates. Colonel Benjamin Arnold commanded the second division, with Captain James Sheldon as junior officer. This division contained two sergeants and seventeen privates as well. Neither division, however, had yet obtained a drum and fife, essential to the coordination of a battle.

As with other colonies, there were many more militia units in the state beyond the Kentish Guard and Pawtuxet Rangers, officially the Second Company of Kent County. Within the collection of the Rhode Island Historical Society's Revolutionary War Papers, an early muster roll of the North Providence Rangers, led by Captain John Angell, includes Lieutenant Thomas Olney and Ensign Joseph Hawkings, along with four sergeants, four corporals, a drummer, a fifer and thirty-eight privates, including Jeremiah Olney, who would rise through the ranks of the Continental Line to become colonel of the First Rhode Island Regiment.

An extensive list also remains of the Smithfield and Cumberland Rangers under Captain George Peck and three junior officers: Lieutenant Nebediah Wilkinson, Second Lieutenant Edward Thompson and Ensign Levi Brown. The list of eighty-eight volunteers includes Stephen, John, Joseph and Simeon Wilkinson.

Brothers Nathan and Samuel Dexter,[27] as well as Simeon and Benjamin Dexter, all sons of Smithfield farmers, also appear on the muster roll. Nathan is listed as a private during the war. Samuel Dexter would serve as ensign of Lippit's Rhode Island State Regiment from August 1776 to March 1777. Simeon would serve as an ensign in the First Battalion of Infantry.

Each company had its own distinct uniform and colors sewn on banners, which were carried by the ensign, usually a man of prestige within the town and a friend of the captain, who chose his own noncommissioned officers.

Colors were an integral part of each community's militia and often combined Puritan symbols of English origin with religious symbolism and some declarative form of liberty. Flags and banners were important symbols and rallying points long before the war with Great Britain, although most certainly grew in popularity as the fervor for a war of independence grew.

Historian David Hackett Fisher believes that the earliest American flags may have been hoisted on the Liberty Tree as early as 1773, if not earlier. These banners had various forms, but their design was of nine red and white horizontal stripes. He cited a similar flag as being the colors of the Manchester militia, a banner made of cotton that was likely carried into battle at Bunker Hill.

Fisher cited other examples of the flags of state militias: "The emblem of Connecticut was an old vine with three bunches of grapes, inscribed *Qui Transtulit Sustinet*—'He who transplants, preserves,' a biblical reference to the carrying of vines into Israel."

This symbol was adapted as early as 1645 to represent the founding towns of Hartford, Windsor and Wethersfield. By the latter half of the eighteenth century, the symbol had branched out to include nine bunches of grapes. Fisher wrote that "above the vines was the puritan symbol of a disembodied hand that represented God's presence in the world."[28] Banners bearing these symbols would be carried into the Revolutionary War.

Rhode Islanders brandished a flag that proclaimed their commitment to "soul liberty," as well as a pure white banner, which carried a blue sheet anchor (the heaviest anchor on a ship, used only in the heaviest of weather to hold the ship fast). This was likely derived from the religious expression popularized in 1642 by Christian philosopher Richard Montagu when he penned the phrase "Christ is the sheet anchor of salvation."

The early flags bore the motto *In te domine speramus*, meaning "In God We Hope." By the time the Rhode Island regiments bore the banner in the Revolution, however, this had been adapted to a blue ribbon emblazoned with the word "Hope."

Uniforms were equally individual. The navy blue regimental coat worn by the Virginia militia since the outbreak of the French and Indian War would be adopted as part of the uniform for the Continental army. But for the

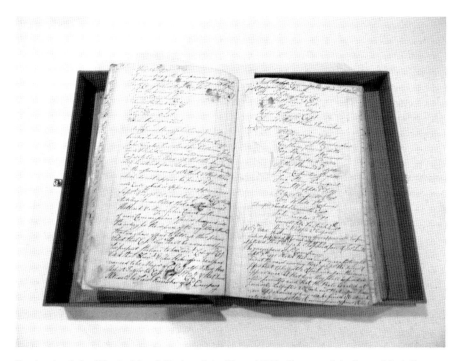

Logbook of the Rhode Island Train of Artillery, 1776. *Courtesy of the James Mitchell Varnum Museum.*

majority of local militia, the preferred "uniform" remained a hunting frock, breeches with woolen leggings, moccasins and a plain, brimmed slouch hat of felted wool.

Virginia's militia had initially adapted this mode of dress during the French and Indian War. In 1755, Colonel George Washington ordered his regiment to adapt the dress for lack of obtaining the regimental coats that were sanctioned to be part of a soldier's uniform. The lack of sufficient clothing, as would be the case in the later Revolution, caused Washington to write to the commander of the Virginia forces in 1758, "My men are very bare of Cloaths/Regimentals I mean/and I have no prospect of a Supply—this want, so far from regretting during this Campaigne, that were I left to pursue my own inclinations I would not only cause the Men to adopt the Indian Dress, but Officers also, and set the example myself."[29]

During the early 1770s, traveler John Ferdinand Dalziel Smyth encountered "longhunters," or men from the mountainous regions of Kentucky and the Carolinas, who would later make up much of the volunteer militia from those colonies during the war. He recorded:

Their whole dress is very singular, and not very materially different from that of the Indians: being a hunting shirt, somewhat resembling a waggoner's frock, ornamented with a great many fringes, tied around the middle with a broad belt, much decorated also, in which is fastened a tomahawk…the shot bag and powder horn carved with a variety of whimsical figures and devices, hang from their necks over one shoulder; and on their heads a flapped hat, of a reddish hue, proceeding from the intensely hot beams of the sun.

This practical uniform would be worn by some troops from the East as well, as seen in the watercolor of the Stockbridge indigenous leader John Nanquim, and was introduced to white troops during the Siege of Boston in 1775. It was the clothing worn by the men from William Thompson's regiment of riflemen of Pennsylvania, as well as Daniel Morgan's sharpshooters from Virginia and Michael Cresap's marksmen from Maryland. It was also adapted by the men of the Rhode Island Regiment and was their preferred uniform through their engagements in the war.

Reenactors of the Rhode Island Regiment. *From left to right*: Carl Becker, Charles Roberts, Keith Kauffman, Dave Cunningham Jr., Norm Desmarais, Coy Bethune and Charlie Walsh. *Photo by the author.*

Prior to the introduction of this "backwater garment" among them, only the garments of the Green Mountain Boys from the region now known as Vermont would adapt the practicality of indigenous dress.

The Continental Congress, both from Washington's pleas and the prodding of Richard Henry Lee, decided after the "insufficient manner in which our soldiers were cloathed" during the harsh winter of 1776 that it must not happen again.

After much delay in finding a suitable American vendor, Lee wrote to the Paris Committee, asking that it find a clothier capable of producing forty thousand "compleat suits of soldiers cloaths" and stipulating that "[t]he coats and waistcoats must be short skirted, to the dress of our soldiery and that they should be generally for men of stouter make than those of France."[30]

What they wore would be but one way in which militias would hold fast to their traditions and community.

Chapter 2

FORGING AN AMERICAN ARMY

At the onset of the Revolutionary War, the colonies turned for their defense to the numerous militia companies in forming the Continental army. Many of the young men who found their unit conscripted into the army were the sons and grandsons of men who had been part of the militia and were recruited from their homes to fight in the French and Indian War.

Their fathers had found that despite the British victory over France, as well as the wide expansion of land this gave the victors, benefits to those who had fought for the empire were few. Many returned home and resumed the hardscrabble life they had left behind on rural farms or as urban laborers, while officers and more privileged veterans secured plum jobs in the city or in government.

These citizen soldiers remained heroes in their own towns, and whether by marching in parades or dressing in uniform for memorial events, they became the embodiment of the historical memory of the war within their communities. The militias thus remained a political and social entity, and it was there that many veterans rose in the ranks.

As tensions escalated in 1774 between Great Britain and its territories in North America, Committees of Correspondence were formed in communities throughout the colonies. These committees worked closely with the Continental Congress and with local Assemblies.

When the conflict with Great Britain grew inevitably closer, militia units began to be formed clandestinely, apart from those still under the Crown, and among whom a few Loyalists might stymie any independent activity. Varnum's Kentish Guard, mentioned in the previous chapter, was one such unit.

The long-held New England tradition of electing militia officers was extended with the creation of companies in New York, New Jersey, Pennsylvania, Maryland and southward.[31] Some local militia leaders saw the assembling Continental army as a threat to their authority and their communities. Up until the time of the Revolutionary War, little had changed concerning the traditions of the American militia units. They elected their own officers, chose the site and times of muster and remained cautious about conflicts outside of their own communities. Historian Holly Mayer observed that "for some soldiers, duty in different states appeared equal to duty in foreign parts."

In New England, with its "strong whig fervor…militia companies not only picked their officers, but sometimes members of a company adopted a document—a kind of covenant—stating their concerns and principles, their rules of behavior, and the limits or restrictions upon their officer's authority."[32] The authority that Congress had given state leaders, therefore, became suspect throughout the colonies.

In Virginia, the dispute grew from smallholders, men who held mainly self-sustaining properties and had no vote or representation in the Virginia House of Burgesses. Those long-held "gentlemen's" companies, which had formed the state militia, were now threatened by the growth of independent militia raised from this segment of society.

At the Virginia Convention in July 1775, delegate George Mason proposed that all the militias be placed under one authority, with officers approved by the state. His proposal received a lukewarm reception, as there were many in the assembly still cautious concerning the idea of a standing army. Mason's plan was only partially approved, recording that a brigade of one thousand men be raised for a state militia, leaving the defense of Virginia to some eight thousand "minutemen" from those smallholder companies.

These men, however, balked at enlisting under that authority. They clung to the tradition of choosing their own leaders, as well as where and when they could muster. These traditions aside, as Woody Holton explained, "The most powerful force keeping smallholders out of minutemen battalions was its enormous demand on their time. New recruits had to leave their homes for twenty days of training; after that, minutemen had to train for another twenty-four days each year."[33]

While many of the elder sons of wealthy landowners throughout New England vied for commissions as officers in the Continental Line, the younger sons were largely content to enlist in the local militia. As their fathers and older brothers were often sent on faraway campaigns, they may well have felt more inclined to protect what was theirs and others' property closer to home.

Wanton Casey of East Greenwich, Rhode Island, was fifteen when he enlisted in the Kentish Guard and spent much of his time during his service guarding the lands on and about an estate his grandmother had inherited. The mansion house on the summit of Casey Hill above the west passage of Narragansett Bay became a favorite target of British patrol ships firing their guns onto the hillside, and at least on one occasion, a fierce skirmish left a hole from a musket ball on a door inside.

Casey would be involved in the Guard's normal duties guarding the shores of East Greenwich, but he was often called on to drive off foraging parties of British coasters that routinely raided farms from Potowomut to Quidnessett, as well as Warwick Neck and Wickford.[34]

Since the *Gaspee* incident in June 1774, the patrolling of Narragansett Bay by British revenue schooners had increased. The infamous Captain James Wallace had patrolled the waters of the bay in the HMS *Rose* since the summer of 1774, and within the next two years, two other patrol ships, the HMS *Glasgow* and the HMS *Swan*, also plied the waters off Rhode Island. The British raided coastal towns and islands indiscriminately, holding citizens at cannon-point to procure supplies that were then largely sent to Boston.

One island in the bay that caught Wallace's attention was the six-mile-long, lamb chop–shaped Prudence Island. Lying an equal mile and a half distant from Warwick Neck to the west and Bristol to the east, the island was long used by farmers to keep their livestock safe from predators. By 1774, thirty-three families also called the island home.

On August 24, 1775, Wallace landed one hundred men on the island and plundered the farm of John Allin, stealing twenty sheep, thirty turkeys and bushels of corn as well as hay. In November of that year, a party of British soldiers landed on the island again, this time raiding houses of clothing and furniture—even a large mahogany desk—as well as two horses and geese.

In December, a skirmish broke out between Rhode Island militia and a British landing party on Conanicut Island. Wishing to avoid another skirmish, Captain Wallace informed the Loyalist governor of the colony that he would be arriving again on Prudence Island on January 12, 1776.

When Samuel Pearce of the Second Portsmouth Company was informed of the British captain's intentions, he could scarcely contain his fury and replied to Governor Joseph Wanton that Wallace and his men would receive nothing unless it came at the point of a bayonet.

Pearce ordered the women and children to be taken off the island and prepared for the coming battle. He had but thirty-two men to protect the island—nearly half from the Allin family—and he hurriedly sent dispatches to Brigadier General William West of the Providence County brigade and Colonel John Waterman, who oversaw forces encamped at Warwick Neck.

The alarm was quickly raised, Lemuel Arnold being among the young men called to the Neck, although initially there were few boats to send men out. Captain Knight had rowed out with twelve men on receiving orders, but it took longer to procure more and for men to gather from the neighboring towns.

As a result, when Wallace landed on the south end of the island in the late afternoon of January 12, Pearce had only 50 men to defend the island. As dusk approached and the British party of 250 troops came ashore, the Americans came forward to engage them. After firing three volleys, the American captains Pearce and Knight clearly saw that the British force was much larger than anticipated and ordered a retreat. Thereafter ensued a running battle into the interior of the island, of which Wallace would boast that his men "beat them from fence to fence, for four miles into their country, firing and wasting the country as we advanced."

Hearing word of the invasion in East Greenwich, Colonel Thomas Fry of the Kentish Guard proposed that the men procure enough boats from the harbor and row the six miles from the town to the island. Wanton Casey was among the men rowed out to defend Prudence Island on the morning of January 13, 1776. The eighty men had just hauled the boats ashore and prepared breakfast when Casey recalled that "while eating breakfast, we received news from a man running very fast, that the enemy was landing three or four miles below us."[35]

Once organized, the Kentish Guard joined forces with troops under Captain James Barton and men from the Tiverton and Richmond regiments of militia. The battle that day lasted some three hours, as the Americans repulsed the British near Farnum's Farm. As the *Providence Gazette* reported, "[T]he enemy several times sent out flanking parties, which were as often driven back to their main bodies."

In Newport, minister Ezra Stiles would record that there was "fireing all afternoon" and that while the British had attempted to surround Barton's troops, the Americans had "repulsed and routed the whole body."

The British forces retreated to their ships, and reports later circulated among the American intelligence that the enemy had lost fourteen men in the battle, nine of these said to have been buried in a mass grave on Hope Island.

The Rhode Islanders left the island that night under cover of darkness. When the British returned on the fifteenth and burned a windmill, outbuildings and six houses, there were no militia sent to defend Prudence Island. It was better to defend the mainland and live to fight another day.

Sixteen-year-old Daniel, the son of Lodowick Updike, then the present owner of the plantation at Cocumscussoc, enlisted in Captain John Brown's company of militia in the spring of 1777. The militia was assigned to Colonel Dyers's regiment. Updike spent four months guarding the shoreline from Wickford, along the length of Boston Neck. He also spent a month in Tiverton with General Spencer's Expedition.

The secret mission under General Joseph Spencer took place in the fall of that first year of Daniel's enlistment. The soldiers for the expedition were called up on September 21, 1777, taking half of Rhode Island's militia, along with militia from Massachusetts and Connecticut. The men were quickly mobilized and trained for an attack by boat on the British-held island of Newport. Due to delays, however, the assault was not fully prepared until October, when a night was finally chosen to ferry the troops from Tiverton to the point of attack where they would take the enemy by surprise.

A mass of boats was collected for the expedition, but on the chosen day a heavy gale blew in, forcing the postponement of the attack. Although the weather continued to be poor, an assault was launched from above Fogland Ferry but turned around when boats were fired upon, the British having gotten wind of the planned assault while the Americans were delayed. In the end, the plan was abandoned, with the general decried for his seeming hesitation on entering battle, although he was later exonerated in the court-martial he requested to clear his name.

The years that followed for Daniel Updike were spent largely the same—several months of guarding the shoreline and a month integrated with a Continental unit. His company served in the Battle of Rhode Island, or what he termed "General Sullivan's Expedition," as well as sudden alarms, a total of what Updike estimated by his account to be "[t]wenty-five months at least of actual military service in said War."[36]

As with other coastal colonies, Rhode Islanders faced a difficult time mustering enough men to defend the many islands and coastal inlets that made up its geography. Fulfilling the need for militia would be a constant struggle throughout the war.

Largely for this reason, indigenous and black men began to be accepted among the volunteers integrated into local militia, even from early on in the conflict. As men of color were still officially barred from service in the Continental army until Rhode Island's Act of 1778, this was yet another declared sign of independence, and such spirit was represented numerous times during the war.

While slaves were officially exempt from military service in Connecticut, it did not prevent them from enlisting in militia units or mustering and drilling in military exercises throughout the tense times of 1774–75.[37] Many of these men of color were among the minutemen who mustered on the alarm after shots were fired in Lexington and made their way to the Siege of Boston.

It was the independent will of the militias that both enlivened and worried General Washington, his officers and the president of the Continental Congress throughout the American Revolution. Washington's charge, as commander-in-chief, was to construct a disciplined, well-trained and well-motivated army to remove Great Britain from the colonies. From his first day on June 19, 1775, he found that he faced a daunting task.

In the war councils that General Washington held during the early spring and summer of 1775, it was decided to "reject negroes altogether" for the Continental army. One of the most boisterous of the officers who objected to black soldiers was General Philip Schuyler, who thought the notion was a disgrace to the army and asked, "Is it consistent with the sons of Freedom to trust their all to be decided by slaves?"

Such was the outcry, however, when the decision was announced in November that the Congress had to backtrack somewhat and allowed free men of color who had experience with military service to be allowed to reenlist in January 1776.

The militias retained those slaves who had enlisted and continued to recruit free men of color during the war. British officer James MacKenzie recorded in July 1777 that when two black men landed on the island and were taken into custody, they told the interrogating officer that free blacks were being heavily recruited in some communities on the mainland.

When General James Mitchell Varnum of Rhode Island proposed an all-black regiment be made from slaves of that state, Washington finally relented; other colonies followed or allowed further integration into their Continental regiments.

Black soldiers from both Rhode Island and Connecticut would serve together at Fort Oswego in 1781–82, under command of Colonel Jeremiah Olney, the leader of the Rhode Island Regiment. Connecticut's Fourth

Regiment, headed by Colonel Zebulon Butler, and Second Regiment under Colonel Herman Swift formed the remainder of the troops in the fort.

The regiment commanded by Butler had been the first all-black unit formed in the state in 1781. As with Rhode Island's regiment, the officers were all white and the privates a mix of men who were black, indigenous or of mixed origin. At the time of Olney's command, the Rhode Island regiment had lost a substantial number of black troops who had enlisted four years earlier when the state had offered freedom for serving the duration of the war. An ambush of the regiment in New York in 1780, and a subsequent epidemic of illness that swept through the ranks while encamped in Philadelphia, meant that the percentage of black troops lost in the Revolutionary War came overwhelmingly from Rhode Island.

Men of color within New England also became mariners for the many privateering vessels that left the region's harbors. The Narragansett and Pokonoket peoples especially were well practiced in navigation and whaling and adjusted easily to life at sea. Black men growing up around coastal ports would have been used to seeing black sailors disembarking from ships that had arrived from around the globe. The acceptance as shipmates and as part of a working society while afloat often gave them more freedom on water than ashore.

While Congress had authorized the formation of a Continental navy, the needed cannons and supplies to outfit ships were slow in coming. What proved valuable to Washington were the mariner corps that had formed among the coastal communities within the united colonies. These mariners were an invaluable resource for portaging men, weapons and supplies along the many waterways involved in the Revolutionary campaigns.

Boys were also recruited for the first time in New England. Where the prospect of a military career was once considered a hard life for men only, with the wartime economy pushing families to the brink of disaster, many boys who would normally have been apprenticed (were the shopkeepers and craftsman not already in the military) accepted the wages offered for their family. As historian Carolyn Cox pointed out, "The presence of boys in the ranks of the Patriot forces during the Revolution may be a sign of the Army's desperate need for manpower as the war dragged on."[38]

Many boys had volunteered as the conflict began; some enlisted with their father or with brothers or cousins in the tight-knit communities of the region. As the lighter muskets and accoutrements were furnished, they became easier to handle by boys grown on the farm and used to performing hard labor. As a result, a handful of these boys would become soldiers.

The HMS *Alert* in Fall River, as drawn by Private Noah Robinson in his journal of November 1778. This ship may be the ten-gun cutter launched at Dover in 1777. The following year, it was captured in the channel by the French, whose records list the *Alert* as a cutter with fourteen four-pound guns. The ship foundered off the coast of New England in 1779. *Courtesy of the Rhode Island Historical Society.*

With the introduction of the drum and fife as instruments used not just for marching in parade but, more importantly, for signaling movements to the troops on the field, boys joined the lines of battle rather than remain servants in camp. While the average age of musicians in the army was sixteen, the enlistment of younger boys was not uncommon.

One such boy was Thomas Mitchell, the son of a farmer, who likely lied about his age when he enlisted with the Rhode Island Regiment of the Continental Line on May 22, 1777, at the age of fifteen. He served under Colonel Israel Angell and performed his duties as fifer at the Battles of Red Bank, Monmouth, Rhode Island, Springfield and Yorktown. The regiment also spent the harsh winters at Valley Forge and Yorktown.[39]

Some were even younger when they enlisted. Fifer John Piatt of the First New Jersey regiment was ten years old when he enlisted in 1776, as was Benjamin Peck of Lamb's Artillery Unit when he enlisted in 1780.[40] Samuel Aborn's son John Anthony Aborn, of Pawtuxet, Rhode Island, enlisted as a drummer at the age of fourteen. He served under General Nathanael Greene, who wrote personally to his commanding officer, General Charles

Lee, from Prospect Hill when the boy became too ill to serve and asked that his father be permitted to escort him home.[41]

Writing that the colonel had "from his public spirit…permitted his Son to enter into the service," the boy was now "sick in Hospital—the Doctor recommends a ride into the Country—the Colonel has brought him a Shaize to carry him and one Thornton home with him, they are both unfit for duty and will be for some time. As soon as they get fit for duty the Colonel promises to return them to Camp—You may depend upon his honor in what he engages."[42]

Men considered too old for soldiering, generally anyone over fifty years of age, were also enlisted as musicians. These boys and men played critical roles in the regiments. In camp, the musicians signaled the activities that made up the course of the day. Drums and fifes were utilized to keep the beat of the march and the morale of the men high as they headed to battle.

Fifers played a variety of tunes, "Yankee Doodle" being the most popularized and associated with the war, although the tune itself had its origins in the twelfth century. A fifer's repertoire was as varied as the musicians themselves. The copybooks that survive from the Revolutionary War include regional dance tunes, traditional European tunes and old English "gavets," as they were called, that were often centuries old. Fifer Thomas Nixon of the Framingham, Massachusetts's militia recorded 104 tunes in his personal copybook during his two years of service.[43]

Drummers learned "rudiments," or patterns of left- and right-hand strokes. These rudiments each had names, such as flams, rolls, drags, flamalues and paradiddles. With such instruction, they learned the different beats and signals for the troops or the call to assemble all noncommissioned officers, consisting of "two rolls and five flams"; the call to send a work detail to collect wood from camp required a "poing stroke and ten-stroke roll."

They were required to learn such signals as outlined in Baron Von Steuben's drill manual, which included "*The General*…to be beat only when the whole are to march.…*The Assembly*…the signal to repair to the colors.…*The Troop*… assembles the soldiers together, for the purpose of calling the roll, and inspecting the men for duty.…*To Arms*…the signal for getting under arms in case of alarm…and *The Parley*…to desire conference with the enemy."[44]

Musicians also wore different uniforms from the regular troops in battle. While the Continental soldiers were outfitted with blue coats that had red cuffs, the musicians were given red coats with blue cuffs to wear. The red coats stood out on the battlefield and identified those who wore them as "non-combatants."

Drum used by Levi Smith of General Nathanael Greene's regiment. *Courtesy of the New Bedford Whaling Museum.*

Woman on the homefront traditionally took on the tasks of sewing uniforms, putting care packages together, writing letters and attending sewing bees and blanket drives for the soldiers. When local volunteers were called to encamp for guard duty, the women of nearby towns and villages often helped to feed the men, provided cooking and cleaning services and sometimes offered their own houses or barns for barracks.

One woman in Massachusetts took on the task of mustering an all-female militia. Prudence Cummings Wright was born in 1740 in Hollis, New Hampshire, where her father, Samuel, served as town clerk. Nearly all of her family was Loyalist, including two brothers, but Prudence would marry David Wright in 1761, then a private in the local militia. In a further break from her family, she joined the Congregationalist Church in 1770.

An account of local history printed in 1899 reported that after the majority of the men of the town of Pepperell, Massachusetts, had left on the alarm from Lexington and Concord, the remaining townspeople had elected Prudence Wright to command a female militia that became known as "Mrs. David Wright's Guard." The militia held thirty to forty women, many of whose husbands had marched with local militia to Boston. They dressed in their husband's clothes and brandished everything from fowling pieces to pitchforks as they marched on patrol.

The women were cited for the capture of British army officer Leonard Whiting as he attempted to cross Jewett's Bridge. He was suspected of meeting with spies outside town, and in one version of the story, Prudence's brother rode with Whiting that night but turned back on the road when he saw his sister in arms.[45] On March 19, 1777, the Town of Pepperell cited the women for their actions and paid compensation of seven pounds, seventeen shillings and sixpence for the capture of the British officer.

Women also enlisted, although they were officially not permitted to serve. The most famous of these was Mary Ludwig Hays McCauley, better known as "Molly Pitcher," the wife of William Hays, an artilleryman of Proctor's Fourth Pennsylvania Artillery. She joined other women who had accompanied their husbands to Valley Forge and did washing, cooking and cleaning for the men in the encampment. They also brought water to them on the battlefield, and therein lies the tale of how Mary Hayes became nicknamed "Molly Pitcher."[46]

Indeed, Washington's army would ultimately comprise an amalgamation of people of varying skills and widely diverse backgrounds. In those early months of the conflict, when fervor for independence spread like wildfire through the colonies, many enlisted, believing that their short term of service would be adequate in freeing their colony from British rule.

The initial enlistments from 1775 were largely extended into the following year, buoyed by the army's early successes and helped by Congress in the form of bonuses and other promises. From Richard Henry Lee's assessment in June 1776, we get an idea of the strength of the army early in the conflict. In New York State were stationed ten thousand regular troops, with another fifteen thousand militia. Troops sent on the ill-fated "Canadian Expedition" included seven thousand regulars, six thousand militiamen and two thousand Indians, and "a flying camp of 10,000" was stationed in the middle colonies.[47]

Chapter 3

A SEPARATE WAR
OF INDEPENDENCE

The Militias Fight to Keep Their Freedom

President of the Continental Congress Richard Henry Lee would initially write excitedly of the militia involvement that he learned of or witnessed himself. On July 21, 1776, he wrote:

> *We learn that the people of Maryland are not quite spectators…but they have attacked and killed some of his* [Lord Dunmore's] *people, and obliged the whole fleet to move its station.…They are continually blasting away at each other.…Last night I was engaged with a party of militia expecting a visit from four of the enemies ships and 3 tenders that appeared off this house about sunset. They are gone up the river, upon what errand I know not, unless to get water where the river is fresh, or to burn Alexandria.*[48]

In January 1777, Lee would write to Patrick Henry that a gentleman had arrived in Baltimore and informed him that the troops in Morristown, New Jersey, were in good spirits, as "the Jersey militia had many skirmishes with the British troops but always beat them. That he met large bodies of militia marching to the Jersies, whence he concluded that the enemy must either quit that state soon, or be exposed to great danger."

On May 3 of that year, Lee would write to General Arthur Lee with news that "the enemy, with about 2,000 men from New York pushed up the sound by water, and made a forced march through some parts of Connecticut to surprise & destroy a Magazine of provisions laid up there for our Army.… However the militia assembled quickly as possible under command of

Generals Wooster and Arnold to the number of about 1500 and attacked the enemy as they were retreating to their ships."

Little did Lee know, as he was writing this, that the incident would stir uneasiness among militia in the field—that while they were engaged far away, their homes and property would be left vulnerable to raids from British foraging vessels.

The Connecticut militia then, despite its involvement at Bunker Hill and other skirmishes for the Continental army, largely refused to answer the call to arms by August 1777, when Washington was desperately trying to shore up the defense of the Hudson River. The commander-in-chief would later condemn the militia's actions, "who because they find no enemy at their doors, refuse to assist their neighbors."[49]

The state would eventually raise a sizeable contingent of men to serve, but only by late September. The persistent problems with recruitment were threefold: protection, pay and provisions. A gathering of the New England Committees of Safety in late December 1776 had attempted to address the hardships placed on the militias with a resolution that stated, in part:

> *Whereas the militia of the several states of New England may be frequently called into the same service, and many inconveniences may be prevented by their being placed upon the same footing in point of incouragement, wages, and rations.*
>
> *Resolved, That it be recommended to the several States aforesaid, that whenever the militia of said States, or either of them, shall be called into service for any term less than two months, that the officers and soldiers be allowed and paid the same wages and rations that those of equal rank in the continental army are allowed and paid. And that it be recommended that when the militia shall be called out for a term more than two months and not exceeding four months, that the non-commissioned officers and soldiers be paid a bounty of twenty shillings; and where their term of service shall amount to five and not exceed six months, that the non-commissioned officers and soldiers be paid a bounty of forty shillings over and above the continental pay and rations, provided they shall voluntarily inlist into such services.[50]*

Despite such efforts to provide incentives and equal pay, those in the militia often felt that such promises paled in the prospects of leaving their homes and families vulnerable to enemy attack.

For Connecticut governor John Trumbull, then, the defense of the colony was foremost in his duties. With an ocean boundary that supported several key ports for the colony that now lay between occupied Newport, Rhode Island, and the tempestuous waters of Long Island Sound, the governor and Assembly were fearful of an enemy invasion on their shores.

The incident that Lee referred to in his letter occurred on the afternoon of April 24, 1777, when two thousand British soldiers landed in the town of Compo, now named Westport, and had marched unimpeded to Danbury by the following afternoon. While the town held some one hundred men in its militia, and another fifty Continentals were stationed nearby, the men had blended in with the townspeople and worked to sequester provisions rather than raise an overwhelmingly outnumbered brigade to defend the town.[51]

Trumbull quickly acted to muster what forces were available. Major Generals Wooster and Silliman mustered their brigades and met with a combined force of six hundred men, and aided by Continental artillery, they succeeded in fending off the British from reaching Norfolk. If it was a victory, however, it was a hollow one. Such a low turnout of militia alarmed the colony. Only some eight hundred men from the western regiments—the Fourth, Ninth, Thirteenth and Sixteenth, whose combined

Illustration of a Connecticut militiaman taken from a poster advertising the author's appearance. *Courtesy of the North Stonington Public Library.*

members numbered four thousand—had answered the alarm.[52]

The need for greater preparedness was at once extant. On the twenty-ninth, the Council of Safety sent the alarm to the four regiments closest to the coastal towns of Groton and New London. On May 4, Trumbull ordered that one quarter of the Second and Fourth Brigades for the defense of the coastline west of New Haven and one quarter from the six regiments stationed in the north and east should guard the eastern shoreline.

That same day, Trumbull wrote to Washington to note that his government was "more in consideration of the Enemy, as it is the great source, among the New England states, of the provisions both for the army and the country; and by their frequent attacks on the different parts, they know they keep us in alarm, and so much divert us from our husbandry as well as soon reduce us to that want which both the army and the country must sensibly feel."[53] He requested two Continental regiments to bolster the defense of the shoreline. Washington could not comply given the poor state of the army. Indeed, the Continental Congress was poor in funds as well.

Colonel G.K. Silliman of the Fourth Connecticut Regiment wrote to his father-in-law, the minister Joseph Fish of Stonington, Connecticut, on December 8, 1777, to let him know of reports he had received that Philadelphia had fallen to the British. He also relayed that many of Washington's officers had offered their resignation, not for the fall of the city but because they could no longer support their families on the pay provided.[54] Silliman confided that General Israel Putnam expected the same request from his officers before the long winter set in.

Silliman wrote, "If the public don't and cant provide some Remedy for this threatening Evil, I fear our Army will be wholly broken up."

Another letter that appeared in the *Connecticut Courant* attributed the poor turnout to the great loss of officers from the local militia conscripted into the Continental Line. Communities lost many of the leaders who roused public response to those crises large and small. Without these leaders, many men felt groundless, with little motivation to fight in distant battles and less inclined to leave their farms and families for weeks at a time.

Coastal communities from Newport to New York were subject to raids from British patrol ships for livestock and goods, the overzealous soldiers often burning what remained in their wake. Connecticut saw its share of these raids—some fatal, as on June 18, 1781, when two men were fatally shot in a skirmish with men from Guilford, one of them being twenty-nine-year-old Simeon Leete, shot while defending the island that bore his family's name.[55]

But the governor's deepest fear would come with the burning of New London later that year. That September saw Benedict Arnold, the former American commander and deserter to the enemy, returning to the country he felt had ignored his talents for leadership. He arrived at the mouth of the Thames River and the gateway to New London, Connecticut, with revenge in his heart and some 1,700 troops with which to exact his tribute.

On September 6, those British and Hessian troops under Arnold's command made their way up the Thames River to New London's harbor. He sent half his force, under command of Colonel Edmund Eyre, to take

Above: The Connecticut shoreline at Sachem's Head, near Guilford. *Photo by the author.*

Right: Gravestone of Simeon Leete, near Guilford, Connecticut. *Photo by the author.*

Fort Griswold, the stone fortification built on Groton Heights, and led the other half in the landing at New London.

The citizens had about seven hours' warning. Sentries at Fort Griswold under command of Colonel William Ledyard had spotted the British vessels on the horizon of Long Island Sound. Recruits had gathered quickly at the fort, and local privateers had sailed upriver to prevent further attack at Norwich.

Arnold and his troops were fired upon as they stepped ashore but forged ahead from the landing and met little resistance as they marched into town. There the troops divided, intending to burn the town from both ends and meet in the center.[56]

The *Connecticut Gazette* would report that on Bank Street "where were some of the most valuable dwelling houses in the Town, the torch of vengeance made a clean sweep." In all, more than 140 houses, shops, ships in the harbor and warehouses were destroyed.

At Fort Griswold, 160 militiamen gathered with a handful of citizens from town to face some 800 British and Hessian soldiers. They bravely refused to surrender the fort and, in fierce fighting, killed a pair of British officers and another 43 soldiers, wounding 193 more.

The Connecticut militia held the fort for forty minutes before it was overtaken. Colonel Ledyard ordered his men to lay down their arms, but after handing over his sword, the commander was run through, and in the ensuing post-surrender slaughter, the enemy troops killed some eighty-three Americans and wounded another thirty-six, some of whom died days

Postcard of Fort Griswold. *From the author's collection.*

later. "Remember New London" was to be Lafayette's rallying cry to the Connecticut troops with him one month later at the Siege of Yorktown.

Pennsylvania had undergone a similar shortage of recruits, with many of those in associations enlisting for short terms and, after a time, resisting those efforts by the state for firmer control of the militia. When the new House of Representatives met under the recently passed state constitution in March 1777, they passed the first militia law in the state's history, mandating under penalty of a hefty fine that all white males between the ages of eighteen and fifty-three must serve in the militia.[57]

As historian Thomas Verenna pointed out, the law "meant that poorer settlers with small families were automatically at a disadvantage, wealthier people could avoid the draft by simply paying whatever was owed, politicians were exempt…substitutes were primarily mercenaries who took advantage of the system to rake in more coin."[58]

Many of those called to service found ways to avoid their obligation. Between 1777 and 1780, substitutes for men drafted for the war made up approximately 42 percent of the militia. Only 7 percent of these substitutes were family members, so others were culled from acquaintances willing to serve.[59] Those poorer and smaller landholders who relied on their farms to be self-sustaining now faced a difficult choice. As Verenna noted, "Each one had to weigh the cost-benefit of showing up for an exercise drill, a muster, and service, or pay a steep fine. There was the concern that a County Lieutenant would force someone's family member to serve in their stead, and the danger was very real in the wilderness. For some, serving tours and showing up for exercises was not worth risking the death of the crops."[60]

Response from the New Jersey militia had also been lax during 1777. General Nathanael Greene wrote to Commander Washington that November, "The Militia of this State is dwindling to nothing. Gen. Varnum says that there were upward of 1400 a few days since, they are reduced now between seven and eight. Colo. Shreeve is gone out to see what Impression he can make upon the People, and to endeavor to draw together as large a number as possible, but I cannot flatter myself with any considerable reinforcement."[61]

Such resistance, however grounded in home and community, would initially cause Washington to hold little faith in the militia. "No dependence can be put on the Militia for a Continuance in Camp," he complained, "or Regularity and Discipline during the short Time they may stay."

General Greene complained in letters that the local militia the army was asked to rely on were "people coming from home with all tender feelings of domestic life…not sufficiently fortified with natural courage to stand the shocking scenes of war. To march over dead men, to hear without concern the groans of the wounded, I say few men can stand such scenes unless steeled by habit or fortified by military pride."[62]

If Washington and his generals were critical of the militia, the president of the Continental Congress disparaged them more and was determined that the war could not be won without forming a standing army to face Great Britain. In September 1776, Richard Henry Lee wrote to Patrick Henry in Virginia that "we still continue here in anxious suspense about the event of things at N. York since the removal of our troops from Long Island nothing of consequence hath happened, but the enemy show by their motions a design to land their army above ours…their design being foreseen, I hope it may be prevented, if the large frequent desertions of the militia do not weaken us too much." He concluded, "The conduct of the militia has been so insufferably bad, that we find it impossible to must be obtained, or all will be lost."[63]

Lee continued to push for a militia-free force of Americans, leading the Continental Congress in instituting a draft, sweetened by a bounty for enlistment in the Continental Line, and not withholding his contempt for those men who remained at home, content to guard the borders and shorelines of their own communities: "I really believe that the number of our lazy, worthless young men, will not be induced to come forth into the service of their country unless the states adopt the mode recommended by Congress of ordering Drafts from the Militia. This may induce the young & lazy to take the Continental bounty, rather than serve for nothing of that sort."[64]

Regardless of Lee's view of "the young & lazy," it was the men with land and voting privileges who now declined to enlist and deferred to stay home.[65]

The Congress approved generous bounties and attempted to raise a "new army" throughout 1777, with decidedly mixed results. The town of Concord, Massachusetts, that of the famous minutemen, was reduced to rounding up "free blacks and other footloose men who could be brought up as substitutes for those who had lost their fire for military service."[66]

The village of Whitinsville, now part of Northbridge, Massachusetts, had a small population of eligible men for the army. The population of the town was 481 men, women and children, and that included 10 Quaker families. In the face of having to fill new quotas, the townspeople voted to pay men from nearby villages to fill out the rolls.[67]

Vermont absented itself from the conflict for two years when the Continental Congress, bowing to pressure from representatives of New York,

Site of the meetinghouse in Whitinsville, Massachusetts, from where the militia marched on the alarm, 1775. *Photo by the author.*

which still held land claims in the courts, refused to recognize the state as a fourteenth colony. As men from Vermont had laid their lives on the line in several campaigns already, the region was grievously affronted and declared itself an independent state in January 1777. The newly named "Republic of Vermont" appointed Thomas Chittenden governor and assembled delegates from towns and counties at a tavern in the village of Windsor to hammer out a constitution.[68]

New enlistees in all the northern states were now mostly men with little prospects beyond apprenticeship—men like Samuel Smith, born in Smithfield, Rhode Island, who was orphaned at thirteen, taken in by a neighbor and fed and clothed in compensation for work on his benefactor's farm. After a year and a half, he was enticed to leave and work for a stranger who offered him a driving job, but he returned after three weeks to his neighbor and worked for room and board for an additional three years. He signed on for another year and was paid twelve dollars. The following year, his wages rose to fifteen dollars for the year, but then his "[m]aster relinquished house-keeping and I was destitute of a home."[69] He fell ill and was taken in by a kindly widow who nursed him back to health. As he regained his strength, "there was a call for soldiers to go to Bristol, and many were drafted to go there, I was hired for one month to take a soldiers place. When that time expired, I enlisted for three months, and when that time was served, I again enlisted in the Continental Army, but was never mustered as a soldier, on account of my right arm being shorter than my left."[70]

Smith would remain in the militia, guarding the Rhode Island coastline, and would eventually be among the recruits detached to join the main army in the Highlands above the Hudson River. From the Highlands, he marched with troops to Red Bank and that "severe battle with the Hessians."[71]

Captain John Billings, a veteran of the Indian Wars and a ropemaker by trade, had moved his young, mixed-race family from Middlesex County, Massachusetts, to the northern territory on Little Deer Island to be closer to his wife's Abenaki family in present-day Maine. The Billingses would be considered the first "white settlers" on the island, and their son Timothy, born in 1764, would be registered as "the first white child born on Deer Island."

Three of Captain Billings's sons would serve: John Billings Jr. would answer the alarm on Lexington and later died from British shelling while building fortifications at Castine, on August 28, 1779, and Lieutenant Benjamin Billings served with the Seventh Massachusetts, enlisting in that crucial year of 1777 along with his brother Solomon, who served in Captain William Reed's company.

Through necessity, the American army evolved from a dependency on landowner-run militia to enlistments of an amalgamation of people who were now woven into the fabric of the emerging nation. Historian Gary Nash aptly pointed out that the mid-Atlantic states were by this stage of the war enlisting a majority of foreign-born men from those Scottish, Irish, English and German immigrants that had poured into those colonies between 1760 and 1775.

So poor was recruitment during that winter that General Nathanael Greene would write from Valley Forge in March 1778, "The States in general appear very dilatory in filling their battalions. The Campaign will open soon, and we should have nothing but the remains of the Army of the last campaign."[72] He had faith however, in the New England militia, and in a letter written on April 25, 1778, he urged General Washington to use them in an attack on New York: "The Militia of New England are numerous, compact, well-armed and equipped and can be easily called out for a sudden enterprise."[73]

Greene would caution in a later letter, with respect to a blockade of Philadelphia, that "[p]ast experience will not authorize an expectation of obtaining such a body of militia for the time requisite....Neither is the temper of militia at all suited to the slow progress of a blockade. We could not reasonably expect from them a degree of patience and perseverance equal to the task; and should be in danger of abandoning us in the most critical moments, obliging us to relinquish the project with confusion and disgrace."[74]

Many states instituted conscription. Massachusetts had established a draft in 1776, and New Hampshire did the same the following year. From 1778 through the duration of the war, the other colonies resorted to the same in some fashion or other.

Once Congress called on the state legislatures to fulfill quotas for the army, the states divided their quotas among the militia regiments, whose colonels would be responsible for procuring men from the muster roll under his command. If not enough were enlisted on a voluntary basis, a common practice was for local captains to draw names from a hat "held by a distinguished citizen who would regularly shake the hat to guarantee fairness."[75]

Despite these seemingly desperate efforts to raise troops to fill the thirty-eight regiments of the Continental army, Richard Henry Lee wrote optimistically in August that "Gen. Gates is reappointed to the Command of the Northern Army and by this time has joined it. The Militia is turning out to join that army, and now that they have the General they can love and confide in, I hope our affairs in that quarter will soon come to better countenance."

While there was an adaptation of discipline and order from militia integrated into the army, the units who stayed behind to answer needed alarms continued to be troublesome to both those officers of the Continental Line charged with their oversight as well as, on occasion, their own superiors. We can look to a few examples that occurred during the war.

In the diary of Noah Robinson, a young private and scribe from Attleboro, Massachusetts, we find a singular incident that occurred while Robinson's company was encamped at Warwick Neck in Rhode Island, along with others of Colonel John Daggett's regiment of the Massachusetts militia.

On a cold first day of March 1778, a young black man came into the encampment and complained that a corporal in an adjoining company from Swansea had struck him. The colonel, apparently believing him to be deserting his company, ordered him placed under guard. But as Robinson wrote, "the company refused, or a part thereof, and rescued him, which caused a fluster in the Regiment. However the rest of the Company was

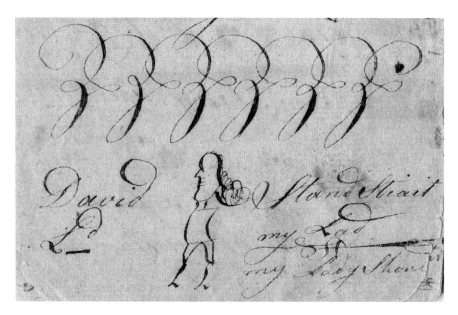

Page from the diary of Private Noah Robinson. *Courtesy of the Rhode Island Historical Society.*

confined & the prisoner taken up." The next day, the "prisoners were all brought before the General and Colonels and those that went to rescue the boy were all confined & the two Corporals put in irons."[76]

The officer in charge of the forces at Warwick Neck was General Ezekiel Cornell. Word of his large-scale confinement spread quickly, and by that evening, he had received orders from General Joseph Spencer, who in civilian life was an attorney from East Haddam, Connecticut, and whose opinion apparently swayed those in higher authority.

The next day, General Cornell assembled the prisoners before the regiment and conveyed the order that "all prisoners were to be discharged from further confinement & their handcuffs be taken off. This was accordingly performed." And then, Robinson recorded, as though nothing of consequence had occurred, "we had a sing."

More common were the mass departures of militiamen when their agreed time of service had expired. The first crisis had come at the close of 1775, when many of the state militias gathered around Boston ended their elected service.

In late November, the Connecticut men who had answered the alarm from Lexington and then enlisted for six months' service under General Charles Lee were apparently all too ready to make their departure. But on the twenty-ninth, the men were mustered and paraded before the general in the doorway of his headquarters, named Hobgoblin Hall, where Lee gave a patriotic pep talk and tried to convince his men to enlist for another year. Some one hundred men agreed, but another three hundred were determined to head home. Some began to leave a few days later, on December 2, a full eight days before their terms expired.[77]

Washington reacted with a hastily written order warning of the dire consequences of desertion. Lee had the men paraded again, this time joined by Brigadier General John Sullivan, a man who would also find his efforts at discipline frustrated by blatant insubordination.

Generals Lee and Sullivan asked the men to stay at least a few days past their time while new enlistments trickled in, but the men refused. According to soldier Simeon Lyman, General Lee then had his soldiers form an empty square, and standing in its center, he bellowed, "'Men, I do not know what to call you; [you] are the worst of all creatures,' and flung and curst and swore at us, and said if [we] would not stay he would order us to go on to Bunker Hill and if we would not go he would order the riflemen to fire at us."

On December 10, the remaining Connecticut soldiers turned in their ammunition, packed their belongings and walked home. The Continental officers were furious, and the troops became the scourge of the letters exchanged in the days and weeks that followed, but Connecticut governor John Trumbull defended his citizens in a letter to Washington. The Connecticut men, he told the general, held liberty in the highest esteem, but "[h]is engagement in the service he thinks purely voluntary—therefore in his estimation, when the time of inlistment is out, he thinks himself not holden, without further engagement, this was the case in the last war. I greatly fear its operation amongst the Soldiers of the other Colonies, as I am sensible this is the genius and spirit of our People."[78]

During the "Siege of Rhode Island" of the summer of 1778, in which American forces strove to remove the British from Newport, the reported fifteen thousand militiamen called from other colonies suffered through delays, a great gale and a shortage of ammunition. A militia unit from Massachusetts had been called up for fifteen days' service and departed once its time had expired, a loss of some three hundred troops before the main battle had begun. Having fulfilled their obligations, and looking ahead to the harvest in the coming weeks, they chose to return home to their farms.[79]

An episode of a more extraordinary nature took place on Boston Neck in Rhode Island the following spring. The Rhode Island militia, in which Sergeant Samuel Smith served, had seen action at Red Bank and Monmouth

The western passage of Narragansett Bay. *Photo by the author.*

before being sent to Rhode Island to join the siege. In the spring of 1779, the men were ordered to leave Warren, Rhode Island, and march to Boston Neck in North Kingstown.

The regiment marched there accordingly, but as they had yet to be paid for their services, the soldiers all agreed to have a letter of concern sent to General John Sullivan. The letter was composed and presented to the colonel, who refused to deliver the petition and placed the man who presented the missive to him in jail. In short order, the colonel had him court-martialed and sentenced to hang within the week

Smith wrote that after roll call three days later, "we agreed on a plan to liberate the prisoner. Every soldier fixed his bayonet on his gun for the purpose of rescuing the brother soldier who was condemned to be hung. The drums beat the long roll as a signal. Every soldier was on parade, with his gun loaded and his bayonet affixed…determined to rescue the prisoner, who was innocent of any crime on behalf of his fellow soldiers." "We were determined to a man," Smith noted, "to lose our lives or rescue our brother."

The soldiers marched toward the encampment where the prisoner was held. They met with General Sullivan, who ordered them to halt, but they pressed on until asked by their own major to halt and confer with the general.

Engraving of General John Sullivan. *From* Lossing's Pictorial History of the Revolutionary War.

Fifteen men were chosen as a delegation, and they marched with Sullivan and the officers to a small island off the road, where they halted to begin negotiations. Initially, the general refused to discuss any terms for release of the prisoner until the men lay down their arms. The soldiers refused to do so until an agreement was reached. General Sullivan mocked them and stated that he had a regiment of black soldiers guarding the fort where the prisoner was held that would "cut them to pieces." The Massachusetts soldiers replied that they were not afraid of him or the black men under his command but would lose their lives, if needed, to liberate the prisoner.

On this, the general finally relented, but he asked that they march back to their encampment; he would deliver the prisoner there. This request the major refused, asserting that he had marched his men there and they would not leave without the prisoner being delivered to them, as well as being given assurances that no man would be court-martialed for the same offense. Smith recorded, "It was apparently hard for the General to agree to it, but at last he complied with the terms and sent an officer for the prisoner, who was then brought and delivered to us. We then marched to our old encampment with our comrade in the center, and colors flying in his hands, and resigned ourselves to our old officers."[80]

Retaining militia beyond their expected term of service continued to be problematic throughout the war, as the lack of funds, clothing and provisions plagued both the regular troops and the local militias. Historian Richard Buell Jr. noted, "By the summer of 1780, the government could no longer offer incentives great enough to overcome the distaste for all forms of military service." Some states, such as Connecticut, began to address what was seen as the insubordination of officers within local militia who refused to draft men when called or disregarded such orders altogether. At least one Connecticut officer openly declared that the quota established for his community was too great to fulfill.[81]

The burden on communities left them scarce of food, men and often medicines or doctors to ease an outbreak of illness. Coastal communities could not guard their shores for the lack of enlistees, and those who were still enlisted in both local militia and the Continental Line continued to vent their frustration.

Glover's Brigade, a band of mostly seafaring veterans from Marblehead, Massachusetts, had contributed much to the war effort, most notably their resolve in the crossing of the Delaware River on Christmas 1776, when they ferried Washington and his troops on their way to Trenton. These men of the sea would prove equally adept on land. In time, as recorded accounts will show, they became legendary among the Continental forces. Throughout the war, the men of the brigade had toughed out the general lack of provisions and equipment. But the lack of pay was what caused most to leave, and they did in increments over the years. Men left the brigade mainly to return to the sea. Those who relished the war signed on as privateers, where some form of pay, in goods or gold, was certain. Others were simply weary of the war, as was their commander.

Glover's departures and returns through the war made it increasingly more difficult to maintain authority. Unlike other commanders who threatened their men into submission, Glover acquired a loyalty from his men based on mutual respect. He would not punish them for harboring thoughts of going home, but he made clear where his loyalty stood—to fulfill his obligation to the Continental army. His men remained loyal and fought fiercely when called on in the fight for New York and at Saratoga.

The winter of 1779–80 saw the men of Marblehead stationed in Lower Salem, New York.[82] By November, while much of the Continental army hunkered down in winter quarters, his men and Nixon's Brigade were still in the field. Glover, who had throughout the war written to Congress concerning the state of his troops, took up his pen once more and wrote to John Hancock of Boston, "Eight hundred of my men are without shoes and stockings…while the worthy and virtuous citizens of America are enduring the hardships, toils and fatigues incidental to parlours, with good fires, and sleeping on beds of down."[83]

Bounty money that the government promised in increments had not been received since the fall. In mid-December, Glover wrote to General Heath that his men had been without bread for several days, and he feared they were on the verge of mutiny.

That act came on New Year's Day 1780, when sixty-nine men, who claimed that their enlistments expired with the close of 1779, picked up their packs and marched out of camp "with their weapons armed and bayonets fixed."

Glover was called from his sickbed to halt the rebellion, which turned out to include not only the men from the two regiments that had departed camp but also others of the Massachusetts Line, leaving their encampments and meeting at a specified location to march home as a single body. Before that could occur, the men were convinced to return to camp by one of Glover's regimental officers.[84] That would not be the case one year later, when the army faced a more serious mutiny from the men of the Pennsylvania Line.

On January 4, 1781, surgeon James Thatcher recorded in his diary, "Reports of a very serious and alarming nature have this day reached us from the Jerseys. The Pennsylvania Line of troops, consisting of about two thousand men, in winter quarters in the vicinity of Morristown, have come to the desperate resolution of revolting from their officers."[85]

Although the troops endured the same hardships as the other soldiers in the American army, the Pennsylvania men felt that they had been singled out and that circumstances particular to themselves justified their revolt. Thatcher's rendering of their predicament, however, sounds similar to the situation other regiments found themselves in throughout the war.

When the soldiers first enlisted, they did so for "a term of three years or during the continuance of the war." The enlisting officers encouraged the men to sign, being greatly of the opinion that the war's end would certainly come before their service expired. But three years later, the war continued. They had received little money, scant clothing with which to face another harsh winter and

A recruitment poster, circa 1776, that would have been posted on tavern walls throughout the colonies. *Courtesy of Wikipedia Commons.*

months ahead with uncertain provisions. At the time of the revolt, they had not been paid anything for twelve months.

The insurgents chose a new commander from their ranks and enlisted nearly the entire contingent of Pennsylvania men but for a small number of men from three regiments. The men paraded under arms without their officers, raided the magazine of ammunition and provisions and seized six fieldpieces. When the officers attempted to raise the remaining men against their brothers, they were fired upon, and the resulting exchange killed one officer and wounded several others, with a few men killed on each side.

General Anthony Wayne attempted to persuade the men to return to duty with the assurances that their grievances would be heard, but to no avail. The men were determined to march to Philadelphia "and demand of Congress the justice that had long been denied them."[86]

The men did just that and commenced on a march to the capital, encamping at night with guards, sentinels and pickets posted about the perimeter. General Wayne supplied them with provisions and also followed the men with several officers to keep lines of communication opened. In this he succeeded, as he was well respected among the troops. By the third day, he had convinced the insurgents to form a committee of sergeants and formalize their complaints in writing. The written claim, according to Thatcher, included the following demands:

> *1st. A discharge for all those, without exception, who had served three years under their original engagements, and had not received the increased bounty and reenlisted for the war. 2nd. An immediate payment of all their arrears of pay and clothing, both to those who would be discharged and those who would be retained. 3rd. The residue of their bounty, to put them on an equal footing with those recently enlisted, and future substantial pay for those who should remain in the service.*[87]

General Wayne could not authorize the demands, but he sent them on to Washington and recommended that they be addressed by the military, as well as civil authorities in Pennsylvania.

Word had reached the British command of the revolt, and General Henry Clinton wasted no time in offering that should the troops continue their march to New York, they would receive their arrears in payment of cash, would be well clothed and with all past offenses forgotten, serving under the protection of the British government.

While Clinton's offer was viewed with disdain, and the emissaries who had delivered the British offer taken prisoner by the insurgents themselves, the American officers worried that the revolt would spread to other regiments "who had equal cause of discontent."

General Washington called a council of war and ordered that five battalions be on the ready to march at a moment's notice. Wayne still hoped for a compromise, and within days, a committee of Congress was appointed that conferred with the Executive Council of the State of Pennsylvania; by the latter's authority, it declared that those who had enlisted and served for three years had finished their tours of duty. Much to Thatcher's disdain, "The result is that the soldiers have accomplished their views, the committee, from prudential motives…complied with their demands, and discharged from service a majority of the line, on their making oath, that they enlisted for three years only."[88]

Within the month, it was learned that a number of men in the Jersey regiments encamped at Pompton in that state had also revolted against their officers. Thatcher wrote that "General Washington is resolutely determined that instance of mutiny shall not pass with impunity."

The battalions placed on alert were sent out at once, with Thatcher accompanying the detachment under command of Major General Robert Howe and Lieutenant Colonel Sprout. He therefore was eyewitness to the justice that would from then on be meted out to deserters and mutineers.

On January 27, around one o'clock in the morning, they came in view of the insurgents' huts. Here they halted and prepared to surprise the men at dawn. Despite some officers' apprehensions that some in the detachment would be faithful in executing orders against their fellow soldiers, Howe ordered the men to be armed, paraded them and spoke solemnly of the crime those men they were about to arrest had committed.

Two fieldpieces were placed in line with the encampment, and the troops surrounded the huts. General Howe next ordered his aide-de-camp to awaken the mutineers and demand that they parade unarmed before their huts within five minutes time. When a second messenger was sent with dire warnings, the men emerged from the huts unarmed and lined up to parade. Thatcher estimated their number to be "between two and three hundred." Despite their numbers, the surgeon recorded, "Finding themselves closely encircled and unable to resist, they quietly submitted to the fate which awaited them."

General Howe ordered that three ringleaders be singled out for "condign punishment." Thatcher wrote that these men "were tried on the spot,

Colonel Sprout being President of the court martial, standing on the snow, and they were sentenced to be immediately shot."[89]

To further the punishment, Howe selected twelve of the most active in the revolt to be the executioners. "This was a most painful task," Thatcher wrote, "being themselves guilty, they were greatly distressed with the duty imposed on them, and when ordered to load, some of them shed tears."

Thatcher concluded, "These unfortunate men have long suffered many serious grievances, which they have sustained with commendable patience; but at length have lost their confidence in public justice. The success of the Pennsylvania insurgents, undoubtedly encouraged them to hope for exemption from punishment. But the very existence of an army depends upon proper discipline and subordination."[90]

Most often violence was avoided in these confrontations between militia and their superiors in the Continental Line. Occasionally, however, such insubordination would lead to unmitigated disaster.

One such example would be that of Thomas Boyd of Pennsylvania. Boyd was part of Thompson's Rifle Brigade, a unit that contained many marksmen, including the notorious "Paxton Boys," who had violated army rules of war during the French and Indian conflict by brutalizing the bodies of their slain enemies.

Boyd had marched with his battalion to Cambridge in record time and took part in the Siege of Boston, and later he volunteered for the ill-fated expedition to Quebec led by Benedict Arnold. He was taken prisoner along with other members of the battalion after their surrender on December 31, 1775.

While Boyd was imprisoned, his brigade became the First Regiment of the Continental Line, also called the First Pennsylvania. Upon his release, Thomas Boyd was promoted to first lieutenant of the regiment, and on January 14, 1778, he was among those chosen for detached duty with the famed Morgan's Rifle Corps with which, wrote a local historian, "he shared the fortunes and hardships of that Regiment in its bloody engagements in New Jersey, Pennsylvania, and New York, and its encampments at Morristown, Middlesex, and Valley Forge."[91]

Through these engagements, Boyd would prove himself a leader. He had come to the command with a reputation for daring escapades, commanding a nearly successful escape while imprisoned, but it may have been that overconfidence, or independent-mindedness, that would lead to an unmitigated disaster.

During the fall of 1779, Boyd's company was supporting troops under General John Sullivan, who was then commanding a campaign to rid the New York area of indigenous allies to the British. On September 13, 1779, Sullivan gave verbal orders to Boyd to take a contingent of five or six men and reconnoiter the area around Little Beards Town, also known as Genesee Castle, a substantial Seneca settlement and British encampment located near the Genesee River.

Boyd immediately disobeyed orders by enlisting a large number of volunteers, bringing his reconnaissance force to some twenty-eight men—a company too large to be inconspicuous and too small for advantage should they stumble upon a large party of Indians. This is exactly what occurred when, in attempting to take a prisoner, his undisciplined volunteers fired upon a small band of Senecas close by the encampment. Within minutes, the men were surrounded and forced to fight to the death, with only Boyd and Private Michael Parker taken alive by the Indians back to Little Beards Town.

The two men were interrogated by British colonel John Butler, whose papers would later attest to their full cooperation. Nonetheless, the colonel and his junior officer left the men to the justice of the Senecas. The American army would find the men's headless bodies the following day, recovering Boyd's head in a bunker but never finding the head of Private Parker.

While nineteenth-century histories would portray Thomas Boyd as a heroic martyr, at the time of the incident, his action was nothing more than that of a rogue militia commander who had disobeyed orders and carelessly led his troops to the slaughter.

SUCH INCIDENTS WERE ONLY a handful of many and are testament to the struggle—from Congress's point of view to maintain a viable standing army and from the view of the minuteman to keep faith in a cause when promises are broken or delayed so long in being fulfilled, when homes and property are left vulnerable because too many men are far from home to defend them.

The militias from across the breadth of the colonies contributed greatly to American victories, and even in smaller skirmishes, they saved or protected countless lives and property. This is why, even with this separate war of independence fought by the militia against the governing body of Congress, the U.S. government would ultimately recognize their contribution in achieving victory and liberty for the colonies.

Chapter 4

A MATTER OF DISCIPLINE

Taming the Militia into a Regular Army

The independent spirit of citizen soldiers often clashed with Washington and his officers' hopes to form an orderly army and oversight of local militia.

The initial Articles of War adopted on June 30, 1775, were similar to those of Great Britain, although the corporal punishment handed down in the American military court was less severe. For instance, while officers in the British army could sentence a soldier to be flogged five hundred lashes or more, the American articles placed the maximum sentence at thirty-nine lashes.

Just one year into his command, however, General Washington wrote that "licentiousness & every kind of disorder triumphantly reign…the little discipline have been laboring to establish in the army, is in a manner done in by having such a mixture of troops."

As with other generals and officers born in the southern states, Washington was uneasy about the men of color within New England regiments, but he also was likely thinking of the legions of untrained and inexperienced young men who had enlisted. In particular, Washington saw the men from New England as dirty, disheveled and undisciplined. New Englanders, in turn, thought the general and his officers bore hierarchal attitudes and were therefore "obnoxious to most people."[92]

While Colonel John Glover's Mariner Regiment (composed mostly of seafaring men that included black and indigenous crewmembers) arrived in Cambridge, they encountered a regiment of Virginia riflemen. The regiments at first merely exchanged mutual shouts of derision—the Virginians made fun of the blue round jackets with leather trim and sailor trousers of the men from Marblehead, while the Yankees derided the riflemen for their hunting frocks and slouch hats cocked at the individuals' fancy rather than in uniform fashion. The exchanges grew more heated and then escalated to a scuffle.

According to the account left to us by Israel Trask, "in less than five minutes more than a thousand combatants were on the field." As the riot spread, Washington rode calmly into the melee, followed by his black servant. Getting close to the instigators, he flung his reins back to his servant, and in Trask's words the general "rushed into the thickest of the melees, with an iron grip, seized the tall, brawny, athletic, savage looking rifleman by the throat, and keeping them at arms-length, alternated shaking and talking to them."

It was a true test of leadership, and Washington would show throughout his command a sense of compassion and decency that few of his officers

Detail from the painting *Washington at Yorktown* by Colonel John Trumbull, as printed in *American Heritage Magazine.* The artist was the aide-de-camp of Washington, and the work depicts the general after the victory while encamped at Verplanks Point on the Hudson River. The original currently hangs in the Winterthur Museum in Delaware. Photo by the author. *Courtesy of the Smithsonian Institute.*

cared to follow. By the end of the war, there were many young soldiers who had faced death but were pardoned by Washington, saved only by the general's intervention.

In this early instance, as historian David Hackett Fisher points out, "The trouble ended without courts, irons, or whips that were more terrible than death to a proud backsetter." Trask wrote in amazement that such hostilities had been calmed in a moment by one man.

Washington was a disciplinarian from the days of his command during the French and Indian War, when he wrote in his journal of 1757, "Discipline is the soul of an army. It makes small numbers formidable; procures success to the weak, and esteem to all." Raised, so to speak, in the canon of British military discipline, Washington would learn to adapt and lead with both discipline and compassion. David Hackett Fisher wrote that Washington "learned that the discipline of a European Regular Army became the enemy of order in an open society. To impose the heavy flogging and capital punishments that were routine in European armies would destroy an army in America."[93]

When a handful of riflemen were found guilty of mutiny, their punishment was not the fate they would face in Great Britain's army. Rather than the death sentence being imposed, the military court handed down fines of twenty shillings to each man, with an appeal to their "honor, reason, pride and conscience."[94]

The following year, some months after Washington's note of licentiousness, new Articles of War were adopted that not only raised the flogging maximum to one hundred lashes but also included a greater number of crimes for which death could be sentenced. These included sleeping while on duty, leaving your post while on duty or otherwise deserting, enlisting with multiple regiments to collect bounties or the "discharging of firearms, drawing of swords, beating of drums or by any other means whatsoever, [causing] false alarms in camp, garrison, or quarters."[95]

Historian Joshua Shepherd noted that the first test of these new articles came from an incident that occurred on September 16, 1776. That day, Washington had sent a detachment of New England troops known as Knowlton's Rangers from Harlem Heights to scout out the British positions to the south. The Rangers, in the course of this expedition, skirmished with a band of British light infantry pickets, and after an initial charge, they were forced to give up their position in the face of a counterattack.[96]

When he heard of the skirmish, the general ordered staff officer Colonel John Reed to round up and send reinforcements. Reed did as instructed, riding out to locate the Third Virginia Regiment and sending the men to support the Rangers, and then he raced his horse to the scene of the fighting. As he neared the scene of the skirmish, he noticed a soldier "running away from where the firing was, with every mark of fear and trepidation."

Reed struck the soldier with the flat of the blade of his sword and ordered the soldier back into the fray. The panicked soldier, one Sergeant Ebenezer Leffingwell of Colonel John Durkee's Connecticut regiment, seemed to comply and ran back toward the fighting. Sometime later, Reed noticed Leffingwell again running from the battle and took chase, brandishing his sword and thrashing at the fleeing soldier until Leffingwell turned and appeared to fire his musket at the approaching officer, although the gun failed to discharge. Colonel Reed grabbed a musket in return from a nearby soldier and continued the chase. He caught up to Leffingwell and aimed his musket. His gun, too, failed to discharge, and in the ensuing struggle, which ended in Leffingwell's arrest, the soldier received a gash from the colonel's sword in the head and suffered the loss of a thumb.

The affair "greatly exacerbated" the Connecticut troops, according to Private James Plumb Martin, who recorded his recollection of the events and the court-martial in his memoir. Leffingwell pleaded not guilty at his court-martial, although there is no record of his testimony. His fellow soldiers, according to Martin's account, claimed that he had been simply following orders to retrieve more ammunition and that the colonel, in his zeal for the fight at hand, had jumped to conclusions in disbelieving the soldier's explanation.

Reed, however, testified at the court-martial that Leffingwell had "since confessed to me that he was running away at the time." The sergeant was found guilty of "misbehaving before the enemy, and of presenting his musket at Colonel Reed; and a breach of the twenty-seventh article of the rules and regulations for the Government of the Continental forces." Leffingwell was sentenced to "suffer death for said crime."

Washington approved the death sentence on September 22, and the execution was scheduled for 11:00 a.m. the following day. All necessary preparations were then made for the firing squad, and at the appointed hour, Leffingwell was marched out before the troops, bound, blindfolded and then forced to kneel while he waited for the command that would cut short his young life.

It never came. Instead, he was pardoned in a lengthy pronouncement read and embellished by a clergyman who clearly seemed annoyed at the overturn of the verdict. When the Connecticut troops heard the pardon, they cheered wildly, and Martin recalled his relief, for he was certain that had Leffingwell been executed, it "would not have been the only blood that would have been spilt" that day.

In his general orders, Washington explained that Leffingwell had been pardoned due to his "earlier good character and the intercession of the adjt. general, against whom he presented his firelock." He warned that "the next offender will suffer death without mercy," and as subsequent cases show, he made good on that promise.

Despite these changes to the articles, an undercurrent of disregard for military discipline continued to run through the encampments of the Continental army, and in some cases more so in the militias left to guard the coastlines and communities vulnerable to British raids and assault. Such an undercurrent—being so prevalent, it seems—came to bear on the army's reputation. The stoic families of New England, however patriotic they might be, were reluctant to encourage their sons to enlist.

John Adams in particular, in a letter to General Nathanael Greene, pointed to a lack of discipline: "There are circumstances which are little attended to, which contribute much more than is imagined to this unfavourable Temper in the People," he wrote. "The Prevalence of Dissipation, Debauchery, Gaming, Prophaneness, and Blasphemy, terrifies the best people on the Continent from trusting their Sons and other Relations among so many dangerous snares and Temptations. Multitudes of People who would with cheerful Resignation Submit their Families to the Dangers of the sword shudder at the Thought of exposing them to what appears to them the more destructive Effects of Vice and Impiety."[97]

Greene shared Adams's and General Washington's view that discipline was key to maintaining order in the army as well as local militia. He was cognizant of the problems that led men to revolt, namely the lack of clothing and provisions that plagued the army until his appointment as quartermaster. Such problems were also why he was an advocate of a regular army from the first days of the war.

Despite popular opposition, Greene persisted in promoting the idea, if at least in private, to his brother Jacob Greene. A letter dated March 17, 1778, strongly asserted, "We must have a good regular army subject to good Discipline, well fed and well cloathed, with a small force; upon such a basis more can be done than twice their numbers, where they are badly fed, badly cloathed, and without discipline."

Greene, in his capacity as general during several campaigns, issued a series of orders concerning punishments, from the threat of confinement for soldiers selling army-issued soap to orders for execution. Punishments were meant to embarrass the convicted and so were meted out in full view of one's regiment. Often the drummer, or a random soldier, was chosen by an officer to inflict the punishment, scrutinized to be sure that each blow was delivered with the utmost exertion. The same occurred on the occasion of an execution, where brothers in arms were forced to form a firing squad and execute a convicted fellow soldier.

The problem was that punishment within the Continental army throughout the war was never consistent. At times, sentences were changed at the last moment or never carried out at all. In other instances, and these unfortunately were more common, officers executed soldiers on the spot or used flogging and other forms of violence to instill fear in the men and bring them to submission.[98]

Some officers of the Continental army did not flinch to execute a man accused of desertion or act as executer of a suspected enemy, whether a trial of some kind had been performed or not. Perhaps one of the more notorious cases concerned the command of General Israel Putnam of Connecticut.

A hero in his local community as a youth for ridding his own and the surrounding farms of a predatory wolf, Putnam served with distinction in the French and Indian War. But Putnam by the time of the Revolutionary War was in his sixties and, by James Thatcher's description, "corpulent and clumsy," but he carried "a bold, undaunted front."[99]

Although seen as a capable officer at Bunker Hill, controversy occurred when Congress appointed him above two other senior militia officers, David Wooster and Joseph Spencer. In the disastrous Battle of Long Island, the general was accused of leaving critical roads open that let the British outflank the Americans.[100]

Washington had given Putnam command over the troops protecting the Hudson Highlands in the summer of 1777, guarding the crucial waterways that connected the eastern colonies to the south, but the performance of his duties fell far short of expectations. There were accusations that the general provided safe passage for Tories and that he let newspapers and perhaps other documents pass through the lines. While these were never proven, his reputation was always in question. And then, in October 1777, Putnam was easily outmaneuvered by Sir Henry Clinton and his three thousand British troops, losing both Forts Clinton and Montgomery, fleeing with his forces and leaving valuable supplies behind to fall into enemy hands. After the

General Israel Putnam, depicted in a British uniform. *From* Lossing's Pictorial History of the Revolutionary War.

American defeat, he was sent back to his home state of Connecticut, where even there he managed to find controversy.

Putnam was a strict disciplinarian. The opening entry in the *General Orders Issued by Major-General Israel Putnam, When in Command of the Highlands…* on June 1, 1777, is the sentence of Private James Murphy, found guilty of "endeavoring to perswade Negroes to inlist in order to join Rogers Rangers—for getting drunk & suspected of going to the Enemy."

Rogers's Rangers were the Queen's Rangers raised by Loyalist Major Robert Rogers of New Hampshire. Murphy received a rather lenient sentence of fifty lashes. William Mitchell, also listed that day, received the maximum one hundred lashes for desertion. Two other soldiers received thirty-nine for their efforts to desert the army. Michael Poor, another private, was found guilty of, among other offenses, getting drunk and "speaking treasonable of language against the States of America." He received "100 lashes on his Bare Back," as did Thomas Cole, a Rhode Islander in Colonel Israel Angel's regiment, convicted of "selling his clothes, that were delivered him from the Continental Store." John Collins, another private who had fallen asleep at his post, was sentenced to fifty lashes.[101]

A little more than a month later, three more men were convicted of attempted desertion. This time, each received the maximum sentence of one hundred lashes. At the same court-martial, John Thompson, with Webb's regiment, was found guilty of "deserting from & inlisting into three Different Reg[iments] and taking Continental bounty.…The Court considering the Circumstances of the Prisoner being an old and worthless person, sentence [Thompson] to receive one hundred lashes and then to be drum'd out of Camp with a Halter about his Neck as a Rogue and Rascall."[102]

Courts-martial were held both at the church in Peekskill and at the "Widdow Warrens," which served as Putnam's headquarters. Punishments were most often meted out in the morning before the assembled troops.

Throughout that spring and summer, while organizing the arriving regiments, the general signed approvals of the recommended punishments, occasionally intervening with the sentence of the court as he saw fit. Putnam strove to cut down on the number of prisoners being sent to the provost guard, the army's military police, and thus brought before court. In the orders for July 2, 1777, we find, "The general desires officers will be more careful in future what Prisoners they send to the Provost Guard, as he finds many are confined there for trifling Crimes, properly cognizable by Regimental Courts."

Still, in the period between June 1, 1777, and November 13, 1777, the troops under Putnam witnessed twenty-five men punished for attempted desertion and thirteen lashed for other crimes, including stealing, selling government property, sleeping at their post or insubordination.

They also witnessed three executions, one recorded on July 1 of the prisoner named John Murray—possibly the man recorded as John Murphy, who was convicted in June. Another was Amos Rose, found guilty on July 22 for "firing a gun loaded with a Ball at Lt. [Elisha] Brewster"; Rose was executed on the same morning as Edward Palmer, convicted of "[p]lundering, robbing & carrying off Cattle, Goods, &c. from the well affected inhabitants & for being a spy of the Enemy." The general sentenced him to be executed "the 1ˢᵗ of next August ensuing between the hours of 9 & 11 in the morning—by hanging him by the Neck until he is dead, dead, dead."[103]

In the "After Orders" entered on July 22, 1777, Putnam lamented the state of discipline among his troops:

> *Considering the Imperfection of Man & his liability to err; The Inexperience & Rashness of Youth that betrays them into many criminal Imprudences & exposes often to be seduced into evil practices by Example of false pretence & subtle Insinuations of designing Veterans in Inquiry & that in some Cases where it would be perfectly just to inflict Punishment, the great End of Government will be answered, the Public Interest Secured by the Exercise of Mercy in the forgiveness of offenders—trusting that all these Reasons concur in the present case to urge & Justify the Hand of Clemency.*

Less than two years later, after being reassigned to Connecticut, Putnam had lost his penchant for thoughtful consideration of clemency, or perhaps he had simply lost his patience. The Connecticut Historical Collections holds one account that demonstrates the elder general's capacity for ruthlessness. The account notes that while "American troops lay at Reading two executions took place; one was a soldier, who was shot for desertion—the other was Mr. Jones, of Ridgefield, a royalist, who was hung as a spy."

The scene of these executions was Gallows Hill, a natural amphitheater that lay about a mile and a half from Putnam's headquarters in what is present-day Redding, Connecticut. Around him were three encampments containing some three brigades totaling three thousand troops. As the community was close by, Putnam decided to make the executions a public spectacle, as well as an example to those troops who might consider the same course of action.

John Smith had enlisted in the First Connecticut battalion, but sometime during his service, the rumors grew that he would flee and join the British troops if he had the chance. When he was found in the woods near Putnam's encampment, it was assumed that he had taken that chance.

Edward Jones was a butcher by trade and a confirmed Tory. When the British occupied New York, he fled his home of Ridgefield to live under British protection. His return for a visit, however, and the suspicion that he had for some time supplied the British with the best of his beef became his undoing; he was arrested and joined Smith in a court-martial presided over by the general. They were quickly declared guilty and confined to a nearby home, where they were jeered by the townspeople as they awaited their fate.[104]

Smith was but a boy of sixteen or seventeen, and when the local minister requested that Putnam appeal to General Washington for a stay of execution, Putnam refused.

On February 19, 1779, the troops were marched out to the clearing on the hill, where a gallows had been prepared. It stood twenty feet high, with a ladder leading to the noose on the platform. The troops lined in formation, and visitors watched from the surrounding hillside.

Jones was led first to the gallows. The hangman having absconded, Putnam ordered two local boys, about twelve years of age, to place a noose around his neck and lead the guilty party to the ladder. Jones was then compelled to climb the ladder, and the rope was tied to the crossbeam above the gallows. He was ordered by Putnam to jump from the ladder. The prisoner refused and proclaimed his innocence again. The aforementioned account describes the horrific scene that followed: "Putnam then ordered the boys…to turn the ladder over. These boys were deeply affected with the trying scene; they cried and sobbed loudly, and earnestly entreated to be excused from doing anything.…Putnam, drawing his sword, ordered them forward, and compelled them at the sword's point to obey his orders."[105]

Smith was then marched some two hundred yards from the gallows where Jones hung and executed by twenty-three of his fellow soldiers. The account reads, "Three balls were shot through his breast, he fell on his face, but immediately turned over on his back; a soldier then advanced, and putting the muzzle of his gun near the convulsive body of the youth, discharged its contents into his forehead."

The body was placed, with Smith's shirt still smoldering from the gunfire, into a plain pine coffin. Then "[a]n officer with a drawn sword stood by, while every soldier of the three brigades, who were out on the occasion, were ordered to march by and look at the mangled remains."[106]

Word of such incidents among the encampments spread like wildfire through the towns and villages where recruiters were scouting out enlistments. It certainly must have reached headquarters. Putnam would be felled by a stroke later that year that would end his military career.

Colonel "Light-Horse Harry" Lee was another officer whose reputation for swift and impulsive judgments seemed to mirror his military actions, which during the war were often impulsive, daring and highly successful. One of the most startling accounts comes from the memoirs of a British prisoner, a Loyalist merchant named Levi Smith, who had been placed in command of the Tory militia guarding Fort Motte, near the Congaree River in South Carolina.[107]

When the fort was overrun in May 1781 by troops under General Marion, Lee was commander of the cavalry and a much more forceful personality than his superior; on the following occasion, it led to outright insubordination.

Smith recalled that the fort was close to the expansive Motte plantation, and after being confined in a local millhouse, he and the other Tory officers, as well as other prisoners, were brought one by one and sentenced to be hanged from the high wooden gates of the estate.

The first to be brought forward was nineteen-year-old Lieutenant Fulker of the local militia, who stood accused of turning a Mrs. Tate of Poplar Creek out of her house "when in the small pox, by which she catched cold and died." The young lieutenant vehemently denied being the cause of the woman's death and "begged he might be brought to trial to make his innocence appear." This was refused to him, and he was told by a cadet that it was "in vain to expect mercy."

And so, Smith wrote:

> *He was accordingly carried to the gate where he was stripped naked and hanged without a trial or even a hearing in his own defense.*
>
> *When he was dead and cut down, Colonel Lee sent the same messenger for John Jackson, a private militia man, and ordered him to prepare for death, accusing him of having carried expresses for the Kings Troops and having killed in action one of General Sumter's men. The poor man begged to be brought to trial, but to no purpose. He was hurried off, stripped, and tied up about dark, and left hanging all night on the gate.*

The next morning, after Jackson's body was taken down, another soldier named Hugh Maskelly was brought before the gate and once more "immediately stripped of his clothes, and an old dirty shirt tied round him, and was then turned off, as the others had been, without the slightest trial or hearing."

Smith, understandably, expected to face the same fate, but as he was called from the millhouse by a sergeant and two privates, who escorted him to the makeshift gallows, he begged the quarter guard to run to his house so that he might see his wife and children before he died. The private obliged him and ran off, leaving him with the other private and the sergeant. As they began the ascent up the hill, the sergeant demanded that he strip. Smith readily gave up his coat but was roughed up and poked with bayonets to prod him until he stripped to his trousers and was escorted to the gate.

An officer rode up on horseback, and taking him to be Colonel Lee, Smith asked him pointedly "if it was lawful to hang a man without a trial and received for an answer that I had got all the trial I need expect to get; that I had acted as a Justice of the Peace, and Militia Officer under the Crown, that I was an enemy of the United States."

He was also accused of taking part in the burning of a house near the ferry but found like the others that "all protestations of my innocence were vain and that no appeal could be made to the Law of Nations." Accordingly, Smith was brought to the gate and forced to wait while efforts were made to cut down the dead Maskelly so as to use the same rope to hang him.

"I had nearly taken farewell of the world, when a sudden noise turned my attention to the outside of the crowd where I perceived General Marion on horseback with his sword drawn," Smith wrote. "He asked in passion what they were doing there. The soldiers answered 'We are hanging them people, sir.' He then asked them who ordered them to hang any person. They replied 'Colonel Lee.' 'I will let you know damn you,' replied Marion, 'that I command here and not Colonel Lee. Do you know that if you hang that man Lord Rawdon will hang a good man in his place—that he will hang Sam Cooper who is to be exchanged for him?'"

As it turned out, a Lieutenant Cooper, perhaps a relative of the Sam Cooper whose life hung in enemy hands, had ridden hard to alert the general to the hangings, and Marion had arrived just in time to save the merchant.

Doubtless reports of these incidents disturbed Washington. He had seen the literally fatal flaw in the Articles of War and addressed it with members, but he finally requested in early 1781 more authority to impose corporeal punishment and thus take the issue into his own hands. The general wrote to the president of Congress from his headquarters at New Windsor, Connecticut, on February 3, 1781:

Sir,

    I have on different occasions done myself the honor to represent to Congress the inconveniences arising from the want of a proper gradation of punishment in our military code; but as no determination has been communicated to me, I conclude a multiplicity of business may have diverted their attention from the object. As I am convinced a great part of the vices of our discipline springs from this source, I take the liberty again to renew the subject.

    The highest corporeal punishment we are allowed to give is an hundred lashes; between that and death there are no degrees. Instances dayly occurring of offfences for which the former is intirely inadequate. Courts Martial to preserve some proportion between the crime and the punishment are obliged to pronounce sentence of death. Capital sentences on this account become more frequent in our service than in any other, so frequent as to render their execution in most cases inexpedient, and it happens from this, that greater offences often escape punishment while lesser are commonly punished, but operate as encouragement to the commission of the former.

    The inconveniences of this defect are obvious. Congress are sensible of the necessity of punishment in the army, of the justice and policy of due proportion between the crime and the penalty, and of course of the necessity of proper degrees in the latter. I shall therefore content myself with observing, that it appears to me indispensible there should be an extension of the present corporeal punishment; and that it would be useful to authorize Courts Martial to sentence delinquints to labor at public works, perhaps even for some crimes, particularly desertion, to transfer them from the land to the sea service, where they have less opportunity to indulge their inconstancy. A variety of punishments is of utility as well as a proportion. The number of lashes may either be indefinite, left to the discretion of the Court to fix, or limited to a larger number; in this case, I would recommend five hundred.

    There is one evil however, which I will particularize, resulting from the imperfection of our regulations in this respect: it is the increase of arbitrary punishments. Officers finding discipline cannot be maintained by a regular course of proceeding are tempted to use their own discretion, which sometimes occasions excesses, to correct which the interests of discipline will not permit much rigor. Prompt, and therefore arbitrary, punishments are not to be avoided in an army, but the necessity for them will be more or less in proportion as the military laws have more or less vigor.

Washington saw the importance of consistency in both the law and in the punishment meted out by the military courts. He knew that while separate from civil mitigation, the courts must also maintain a continuity of law, where every man accused was given representation and their day in court.

PART II

SELECTED CONTRIBUTIONS OF MILITIA TO THE REVOLUTIONARY WAR

Chapter 5

THE RIFLEMEN BRIGADES

When New York governor George Clinton put out an urgent request for assistance in the Upstate territories threatened by British and Indian allies, the commander-in-chief dispatched three hundred troops, including two companies of riflemen. The brigade came under command of Colonel William Butler of the Fourth Pennsylvania Regiment.

These men were recruited from those militias mentioned in the last chapter, whose origins were in the frontiers of Pennsylvania, Virginia and Maryland. The band gathered from those riflemen may be considered the first official soldiers of the new American army.[108] Equipped with long rifles, so called for the grooves or "rifling" inside the barrel that gave the ball greater speed and accuracy than the common smoothbore musket, the men prided themselves on their weapons and marksmanship.

In September 1775, three rifle brigades were chosen to lead the expedition to Quebec under Colonel Benedict Arnold. Captains William Hendricks of Pennsylvania, Daniel Morgan of Virginia and Matthew Smith of Thompson's Rifle Brigade would lead their men and be joined by volunteers from New England, mostly from Rhode Island and Connecticut, who would follow these troops through the wilderness with supplies and ammunition.

One contingent of troops, before leaving the town of Newburyport, Massachusetts, attended Sunday service at the First Presbyterian Church and listened to a sermon from minister Samuel Spring. Knowing that the famed British evangelical George Whitefield was buried in a vault beneath the church, one of the parties inquired about a visit, which was quickly arranged for their benefit. The sexton led the soldiers down to where the coffin lay; once there "the officers induced the sexton to take off the lid of the coffin…some portions of his grave-clothes remained His collar and wristbands, in the best preservation, were taken and carefully cut in little pieces and divided among them."[109]

From Fort Western in present-day Augusta, Maine, the men navigated the Kennebec River, portaging heavy wooden boats around the falls at Norridgewock and Skowhegan. They next navigated the Dead River and a series of ponds before beginning a long trek through the wilderness of Canada.

Spearheading the campaign, they were assigned with the task of "ascertaining and marking the paths, used by the Indians at the numerous carrying-places in the wilderness…and also, to ascertain the course of the river Chaudiere, which runs from the height of land, towards Quebec."[110]

A group of five riflemen from the three companies under Lieutenant Archibald Steele of Smith's company set out with a pair of local guides in two "light barks," or birchbark canoes. These men made five or six miles per day, followed closely by the remainder of the rifle brigades. So quickly did these men move through the wilderness that the New England troops soon fell far behind. Surgeon Isaac Senter from Newport, Rhode Island, noted that the "forward Division of Riflemen…were better acquainted…with the disadvantages of life in the woods as well as this kind of inland navigation than the New England troops who made up the two rear ones."[111]

The rest of the troops made their way as best they could, with Senter writing, "We have…illy adapted these large & heavy boats were (?) against a stream…in this stage which mostly ran not much short of three miles an hour & in many places much more—in where much skill as well as strength was required—in the former we generally failed, for very few of the men have ever been acquainted with [this] kind of savage navigation."[112]

Indeed the remainder of the troops would go through weeks of hardship and uncertainty, as evidenced in just a few passages from the journal of Colonel John Topham of Newport, Rhode Island. By the end of October, the situation for the crestfallen troops from New England seemed dire:

> October 20
> "It rained very hard, our boats not having come up…here we staid the night, it being the 3rd day that we have been obliged to lay by for provisions."
>
> October 21
> "It rained very hard and was almost as heavy a storm as I ever saw.… Major Bigelow, who had been down with the boats, returned with

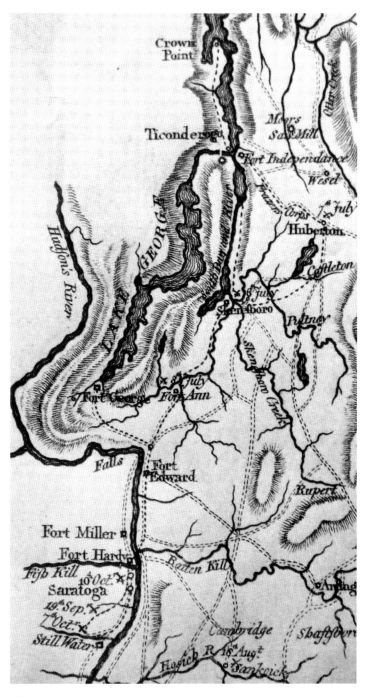

Map of the northern territories. *From Carrington's* Battles of the American Revolution.

only a barrel of flour, we are very short of provisions & there is no probability of getting any more, we have no other view than either to proceed to Canada or to retreat, here we concluded to send back those men who were not able to do actual duty, the river since last night has risen 2 feet and a half which occasions the river to run very swift, our encampment grew very uncomfortable especially for those who have no tents."

When the storm abated, the men proceeded up the river, moving against what was estimated to be at least a five-mile-per-hour current. It was exhausting work, wet and cold. The men were heading to a height of land they would have to climb through thick woods to reach.

OCTOBER 24
"Received accounts of it being 25 miles to height of land, and we are almost destitute of provisions, being brought to ½ pint of flour per man and having no more to deliver out, it being the last we have."

The weather grew colder and brought snow. Colonel Christopher Greene was sent forward to see what could be done about securing provisions from the French. Topham wrote that "we are in absolute danger of starving, however I hope for the best, but if we do not receive a supply from the French, we shall be poorly off."

The French promised provisions and sent pilots to help guide the men, but these were soon found to be unfamiliar with the territory and leading the men only by guesswork. The men slogged on, and Topham noted that one man, Samuel Nichols, "who must inevitably perish with hunger," was still among them. On the thirty-first, they came upon a few wrecked boats along the river and the body of one drowned rifleman, as well as another of the battalion left behind in sickly condition.

NOVEMBER 1
"Proceeded again, our people grew very much fatigued and begin to fall in the rear, being much reduced with hunger and cold, I saw with astonishment, a dog killed, and even his haunch, guts, and skin eaten."

NOVEMBER 2
"Proceeded…through much fatigue, went about 16 miles, it is an astonishing thing to see almost every man, without any sustenance

but cold water, which is much more weakening than strengthening, I have now been 48 hours without victuals."

NOVEMBER 3
"Proceeded and met a party with beef and oatmeal which was never sifted, this I thought was as good bread as I ever eat."

That night, they reached a house and barracked but apparently did not receive any provisions. Two days later, the troops reached another house.

NOVEMBER 5
"Proceeded 5 miles to another house, where provision was made for the army, the inhabitants…are very civil, but they ask a prodigious price for what they have to sell."

The following day, they marched another fifteen miles to a church, where the minister "spared everything that he could."[113]

Thankfully, Colonel Christopher Greene and Arnold had moved ahead and secured some cattle and other provisions. As the men regrouped and worked their way toward Quebec, Morgan's men in the advance would prove indispensable as a hunting party, "who kept in front of all the other troops for the purpose of taking all the wild game they could."

When they reached Quebec, Arnold's fatigued army was forced to wait for the arrival of troops under General Montgomery. The task they faced was daunting. The fortified city lay on a high, jagged peninsula that stretched out into the intersection of the St. Lawrence and St. Charles Rivers. Lower Town, as it was called, dotted the curving coastline at the end of the peninsula, while above, at the summit of the cliff, stood Upper Town, protected by the steep rock on three sides and on the west by a thirty-foot wall that extended from one river to the other.

The decision was made to storm the city, and Arnold, along with Daniel Morgan as second in command, led some six hundred troops and attacked from the northern side of Lower Town. Montgomery took another three hundred men and led an assault from the south. As with the best-laid plans, things went wrong from the beginning of the expedition. Rhode Islander William Humphrey recorded in his diary on the night of December 30:

[T]his evening about 10 o'clock received orders that it was the general determination to storm the city of Quebec; then we ordered our men to get

their arms in readiness for to go and storm; it was very dark and snowed. We were to receive a signal by 3 skyrockets when to attack, but not observing them, we was about ½ hour too late; Capt. Dearborne's Company, on account of being quartered on the other side of the [St.] Charles River and tide being high, not coming up, however, we proceeded without them.

Arnold, meanwhile, had succeeded with the aid of Morgan's riflemen in advancing to the barricades on the northern end of Lower Town. His force included riflemen from Virginia and Pennsylvania, as well as the volunteers from Rhode Island[114] and other parts of New England. Canadians and indigenous allies also joined in the attack on Quebec.

Artillery had drawn up a six-pounder cannon on a sled, but high drifts made keeping up with the advancing riflemen difficult and it was finally abandoned under fire. Arnold soon found himself and his men under heavy fire from above. Grenades were hurled down at the riflemen as they attempted to return fire at their assailants on the summit of the mountainous walls. Arnold directed the men toward the docks of the city, which were unprotected by the walls. It moved them from harm's way momentarily, but the troops were as unfamiliar with the streets of Quebec City as if they had been dropped in St. Petersburg, and the men soon became lost in the maze of blocks of cobblestone lanes and tall houses, all blurred amid the blizzard that continued to fall.

The Americans came under fire again when they advanced down a narrow street toward a barricade that held three light cannons and a contingent of thirty Canadian militia. As he attempted to organize a frontal assault, Arnold was wounded in the leg and was quickly carried from the scene. Rifleman Daniel Morgan took command and led the assault on the barricade. It is written that he scaled a ladder once and was knocked back, but on the second attempt, he rolled under one of the cannons onto the barricade and his men quickly followed.

They succeeded in taking the barricade and took the Canadians prisoner. Still, they were in an unpredictable situation. A brave but brief effort to take a second barricade drove the men back to the shelter of some houses. Morgan and his men still knew nothing of what had happened to Montgomery and his forces, and exposing themselves in the narrow streets while their powder was wet and unusable left them defenseless. Despite Morgan's own eagerness to advance the attack, he agreed to hunker down in buildings to dry powder and rearm before they advanced again.

Humphrey would record that "when we came out we found we could not retreat without losing all our men or at least the most of them."[115]

Dearborn's company attempted to come to the riflemen's aide but had to surrender when the men's weapons also failed.

The Highlanders pinned Morgan's men down in a handful of houses and blocked any effort the Americans made to rally and escape under fire. Eventually, they ran out of ammunition and were forced to surrender, with Morgan handing his sword to the Catholic priest who had been sent with terms of surrender rather than hand it over to a British officer.

Daniel Morgan was among the 372 men captured and taken prisoner. He would be released in January 1777 and promoted to colonel. He was then given command of a new regiment of the Continental Line, the Eleventh Virginia, consisting once again of marksmen chosen from Pennsylvania, Maryland and Virginia regiments.

On January 1, 1776, Colonel Thompson's Battalion of Riflemen became the First Pennsylvania, or First Regiment of the Continental Line.

The regiment left Cambridge with those other troops under General John Sullivan and headed for the defense of New York.

The First Pennsylvania guarded the coastline of Long Island, during which, as Richard Henry Lee wrote, "the riflemen here had a fair engagement with a small man of war for the watering place at N. York, when the former drove the latter off, and have since fortified the spring, so that they [the British] must go somewhere else for water."[116]

Such was their performance in the field that Washington wrote to the president of the Continental Congress in the spring, "The time for which the riflemen enlisted will expire July 1st, and as the loss of such a valuable and brave body of men will be of great injury to the service, I would submit to the consideration of Congress whether it would not be best to adopt some method to induce them to continue."

Lee knew well their reputation. In fact, he had written glowingly of these men to General Arthur Lee little more than a year earlier:

> *The inclosed Address to the Virginia Delegates published a few days since in the Gazette will shew you the spirit of the Frontier Men—This one County of Fincastle can furnish 1000 Rifle Men that for their number make the most formidable light infantry in the World. The six frontier Counties can produce 6,000 of these Men who from their amazing hardihood, their method of living so long in the woods without carrying provisions with them, the exceeding quickness with which they can march to distant parts,*

and above all, the dexterity to which they have arrived in the use of the Rifle Gun. There is not one of these Men who wish a distance less than 200 yards or a larger object than an Orange—Every shot is fatal.[117]

The First Pennsylvania was sent to Delancey's Mills in August 1776 and encamped three miles above King's Bridge. The men successfully fended off attempted landings from enemy troops but were withdrawn before the disastrous Battle of Long Island, in which their marksmanship might have made a difference in the outcome. They were, however, with Washington again during his famous Christmas Day attack on Trenton, New Jersey.

Washington began planning the assault on the brigade of some 1,500 Hessians entrenched in the village by assembling a council of war on December 22. The general's plan of attack included dividing the 3,000 troops at his disposal into two columns. The largest force, which included some 2,400 Continentals and eighteen artillery pieces, would be ferried across the Delaware River eight miles above the village and then make its way from the north and east to the village. Another column of mostly militia would seal off Trenton from the south and prevent any reinforcements from nearby Brandontown coming to the Hessians' assistance.[118]

As a snowstorm began around 4:00 p.m. Christmas Day, the first column began to be ferried across the river by members of Glover's Fourteenth Continental Brigade, made up of men mostly from Marblehead, who were familiar with wintry conditions on the water. All night the men broke chunks of ice with pikes and oars to get the men across the Delaware. A young field officer on Washington's staff named John Fitzgerald recorded in his journal from the ferry house on the New Jersey side, "I have never seen Washington so determined as he is now. He stands on the bank of the river, wrapped in his cloak, superintending the landing of his troops. He is calm and collected, but very determined. The storm is changing to sleet and cuts like a knife. The last cannon is being loaded and we are ready to mount our horses."[119]

By 4:00 a.m., only two of the four divisions had been ferried across, and they were more than three hours behind schedule. But Washington formed the men into a column along the riverbank and began the march.

The two divisions divided at Bear Tavern and reached the outskirts of the village at daybreak. Washington stopped his troops at the home of a man chopping wood, who directed them to the house where the Hessian command was billeted. Within minutes, the German troops were struggling to assemble a defense, recalled in Fitzgerald's account:

We could see a great commotion down toward the meeting house, men running here and there, officers swinging their swords, artillerymen harnessing their horses. Captain Forrest unlimbered his guns. Washington gave the order to advance, and we rushed on to the junction of King and Queen Streets. Forrest wheeled six of his cannon into position to sweep both streets. The riflemen under Colonel Hand, and Scott's and Lawson's battalions, went upon the run through the fields on the left to gain possession of the Princeton road. The Hessians were just ready to open fire with two of their cannons when Captain Washington and Lieutenant [James] Munroe with their men rushed forward and captured them.[120]

The German forces were routed. Their veteran commander, having drunk and eaten heartily at the Trenton Tavern on Christmas Day, was awakened from his bed, only to be mortally wounded within minutes of mounting his horse.

After recrossing the Delaware on the twenty-seventh and returning to headquarters, Washington learned that he had been granted executive war powers, as he had long requested from Congress. In short order, he

The Battle of Trenton, as illustrated in *American Heritage Magazine. Courtesy of the Smithsonian Institute.*

assembled the troops, exhausted but still flush with victory, and exhorted them to extend their periods of enlistment. The arrival of supplies and hard currency boosted the men's morale and helped sway those who might have hesitated about signing up for several more weeks.

The end result was that Washington found himself with the strongest army he had yet possessed: some 3,335 Continentals at his encampment, with another 3,000 men stationed in New Jersey. He took immediate advantage, although the risk was great. Hearing of the debacle at Trenton, British general Cornwallis marched the 8,000 troops under his command on January 2, 1777, and attempted to blockade the Americans in the town.

The Pennsylvanians were among the militia that helped to slow Cornwallis's entire army to a crawl at Five Mile Run and along the bank of Assunpink Creek as it led to the Delaware.

At 2:00 a.m. on the third, Washington led his troops along the icy road past the Barrens to Quaker Bridge, with a small contingent left behind in Trenton to keep the campfires lit and the British guessing as to their numbers. The Americans slipped through the loose blockade that Cornwallis had managed to put in place and attacked the general's rear detachment just past Bear Swamp, roughly two miles from Princeton.

At the Battle of Brandywine, the regiment was aligned with Colonel Thomas Hartley's First Pennsylvania Brigade and led in the battle by Colonel James Chambers. They fought near Chadds Ford under General Anthony Wayne, holding the far-right flank of the division, and at the Battle of Germantown, where they were brigaded with the Second, Seventh and Tenth Pennsylvania Regiments.

Surgeon James Thatcher recorded their appearance in battle and the deadly accuracy they held with the long rifle:

> They are remarkably stout and hardy men; many of them exceeding six feet in height. They are dressed in white frocks or rifle shirts and round hats. There men are remarkable for the accuracy of their aim; striking a mark with great certainty at two hundred yards distance. At a review, a company of them, while in a quick advance, fired their balls into objects of seven inches diameter at the distance of 250 yards…their shot have frequently proved fatal to British officers and soldiers who expose themselves to view at more than double the distance of common musket shot.

The First Pennsylvania Regiment would see action at Matson's Ford, a crossing at the Schuylkill River in present-day Conshohocken, Pennsylvania.

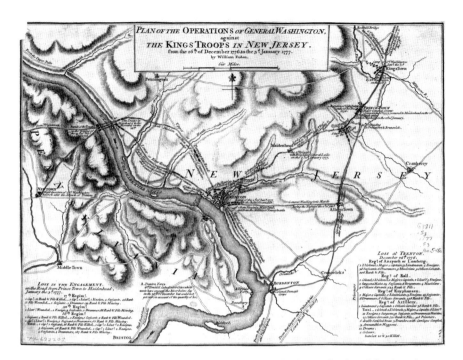

Map detailing Washington's campaign in New Jersey. *From Carrington's* Battles of the American Revolution.

As the Continental army prepared for winter quarters west of the river, Washington sent the Pennsylvania militia, under command of General James Potter, to advance ahead of the troops and establish three pickets west of the river, at Middle Ferry, another crossing on the river; one at the Black Horse Inn, situated on the Old Lancaster Road; and the third at Harriton House on Old Gulph Road, then the residence of Charles Thompson, who was secretary to the Continental Congress.

Unbeknownst to the Americans, a sizeable force under General Cornwallis had set out to forage along the riverbank. This included brigades of light infantry, two troops of dragoons, a detachment of German Jägers and one brigade of infantry. They pulled with them half a dozen six-pound cannons. The British attempted a crossing at Middle Ferry and quickly came under musket fire. The force retreated and began moving down the road toward Matson's Ford. Soon after, the militia at the Black Horse Inn came under heavy fire.[121]

The militia fell back, taking heavy casualties and sending a runner urgently to warn General Potter of the British advance. Potter would place five regiments of militia to face the forces heading toward Harriton House.

Despite "a stubborn resistance," the militia was eventually sent into retreat, scattering their weapons and ammunition as they fled. Captain Johann Ewald determined that the British captured 160 men.[122] With the militia dispersed, Cornwallis abandoned any pursuit of the Americans but stationed his troops on a rise above the river overlooking Matson's Ford.

The following day, unaware of the British position, two regiments under General John Sullivan began building a temporary bridge with wagons lashed together to attempt another crossing. They were nearly finished when the British were spotted on the rise opposite, and they were forced to retreat, destroying the makeshift bridge as they moved back across the Schuylkill.

The Continental army remained encamped in the hills above Swede's Ford while scouting parties reconnoitered the British forces across the river. Finding the troops already gone, on the evening of December 12 the Americans again lashed wagons together and made a temporary bridge that allowed them to cross the river and march down Swedeland Road to an area called Gulph Mills, where they encamped for another week. On December 18, the first national holiday in the new nation was declared a day of "Thanksgiving and Praise" to celebrate the American victory at Saratoga.

The following morning of December 19, the Continental army marched the seven miles to Valley Forge, where it made its winter quarters.

The First Pennsylvania would also participate in battles at Monmouth, New Jersey, the following year and Springfield in 1780. The soldiers of the unit were furloughed on June 11, 1783, at Philadelphia and officially disbanded on November 15, 1783.

In the spring of 1777, General Washington chose Daniel Morgan of the Eleventh Virginia to form another regiment of riflemen. Recruitment was slow, due to the standards for marksmanship that Morgan had set, as well as his apathy toward those who deferred to enlist. By late March, he had raised 180 marksmen and, with these, set out for Washington's encampment. The corps stopped briefly in Philadelphia to be inoculated against smallpox before marching on to Morristown, New Jersey.

Morgan gathered more men from widely scattered regiments. He named two junior officers in Lieutenant Colonel Richard Butler and Major Jacob Morris. Eight companies were under his command, with the quota of officers and men being Pennsylvania, 193; Virginia, 163; Maryland, 65; and 87 from other states, for a total of 508 men.[123]

Once in New Jersey, Morgan's Corps of riflemen soon found itself actively engaged, ambushing the British on the Amwell Road in Somerset on June

The Battle of Princeton, as illustrated in *American Heritage Magazine. Courtesy of the Smithsonian Institute.*

14. A week later, it joined with regular troops in dislodging a German picket outside New Brunswick and chased the Hessians all the way to Piscataway.

The corps was next dispatched to the Highlands above the Hudson River. The riflemen were a fleet regiment, able to cover lots of ground in a short time, and perfect for the mission Washington had sent them on—to reconnoiter for any advancement of Howe and Cornwallis's troops, which he feared might rendezvous and form a large advancement against the American encampment at Albany.

Morgan's Corps, then, was sent on a circuitous route to Philadelphia and on to Trenton, Germantown, Maidenhead and then Trenton again. In August 1777, they were with the troops commanded by General Horatio Gates and contributed to slowing Burgoyne's march to a crawl in New York State. After the repelling of Burgoyne, the riflemen were carried in three boats to Albany.

The rifle corps' actions during the fall of 1777 would make it a "corps of celebrity" among the troops. The men spent much of their time patrolling the surrounding woods, skirmishing with Indian scouts, destroying cattle and horses to keep them from falling into enemy hands and proving the deadly accuracy of their marksmanship once again in the Battle of Freeman's Farm on September 19.

Just as with the Pennsylvania riflemen, the Virginians under Morgan would leave their own mark on the battles at Saratoga. Although the outcome of the first battle was indecisive, the heavy losses incurred for the British forces were largely due to Morgan's Corps picking off officers and artillery; some historians have claimed the riflemen were responsible for half of the six hundred men the enemy lost that afternoon. An eyewitness account left by Frank Moore recalled:

> *Yesterday, about noon, the two armies met near Stillwater, and a most obstinate and bloody battle ensued. The advanced parties of the Americans, which were composed of Morgan's riflemen and Dearborn's infantry, received the first fire of the enemy, and a little after two o'clock the action became general....By turns the British and Americans drove each other, taking and retaking the field, pieces, and often mingling in a hand to hand wrestle and fight....At sundown the action was less furious, and a little after dark a greater part of the two armies retired from the field. Some of our men did not come off until near midnight.*[124]

The battle also caused a rift between General Horatio Gates and Major General Benedict Arnold. So heated were their disagreements that Gates

"Where the battle began," Saratoga, New York. *Photo by the author.*

Cannon at Bemis Heights, Saratoga, New York. *Photo by the author.*

relieved Arnold of his command. It was in the aftermath that Daniel Morgan conferred with Gates and advised him of a plan for the next encounter with the British at Bemis Heights.

After gaining ground at Freeman's Farm, the British spent a week fortifying their position while the Americans regrouped just north at Bemis Heights above the river. On October 7, Burgoyne sent out three columns to survey the American encampment, and with Morgan's advisement, Gates initiated a three-pronged assault, with Morgan's men attacking from the west, Poor's Brigade from the east and the Continental Brigade, under command of Colonel Ebenezer Learned, striking at the center of the columns.

James Thatcher recorded, "The gallant Colonel Morgan, at the head of his famous rifle corps, and Major Dearborn, leading a detachment of infantry, commenced the action, and rushed courageously on the British grenadiers, commanded by Major Ackland; and the furious attack was most firmly resisted."

As the British attempted to regroup, one of Morgan's men named Timothy Murphy was assigned to climb into a tree and act as a sniper in support of the ground troops. Murphy was likely the best shooter available to Morgan, and the list of heroic deeds attributed to him was long before the battles at

Left: Monument to rifleman Timothy Murphy, Saratoga, New York. *Photo by the author.*

Right: "Here Frazer Fell," Saratoga, New York. *Photo by the author.*

Saratoga. Among those who fell under Murphy's fire were British general Simon Fraser and his aide, who were mortally wounded as they attempted to rally their regiment. Around the same time, seeing the weakness in the British defenses, Major General Arnold charged on horseback to the line and took command of Learned's Continental Brigade, pressing the enemy's center column back and separating the gathering units.

Thatcher noted his officer's accounts:

> *He entered the field…and his conduct was marked with intemperate rashness; flourishing his sword and animating the troops, he struck an officer on the head without cause, and gave him a considerable wound. In the heat of the action, when our troops were gaining advantage, he ordered Lieutenant Colonel Brooks, at the head of his regiment, to force the German lines, which was instantly obeyed, and they boldly entered at the sally port together, where Arnold received a wound in his leg, and his horse was killed under him.*[125]

Morgan led men on to attack a pair of British redoubts built in the past week, eventually forcing them back to their positions at Freeman's Farm. Following

Burgoyne's surrender at Saratoga, the riflemen rejoined Washington's army, which now lay at Whitmarsh, Pennsylvania. Although they had helped to secure a much-needed victory for the American forces, the rifle corps were so depleted by casualties from the battle, as well as illness and inertia that had taken hold of so many, that only 175 men were deemed fit for duty.

Some of these served under the Marquis de Lafayette during an attack on a German picket near the Delaware River that drove the Hessians one mile farther into the woods. Others of the rifle corps took part in the Battle of White Marsh in early December 1777.

Morgan's riflemen spent much of that winter reconnoitering, often capturing deserters from the enemy or skirmishing with foraging parties from the British encampments. They chased British general Henry Clinton's troops departing from Philadelphia in June 1778, pursuing them "across the Jerseys" and taking some one hundred deserters and thirty prisoners.[126]

Poor communication prevented the riflemen's participation in the Battle of Monmouth, but they quickly moved to protect communities along the British general's path of retreat, skirmishing with British detachments that would have devastated communities.

The rifle corps rejoined General Washington's encampment at White Plains, New York, and for a time patrolled the shoreline of Westchester County, across the Hudson River from the enemy stronghold on Manhattan Island.

In July 1778, Morgan was named to command the Seventh Virginia Regiment and relinquished command of the rifle corps. The corps was then disbanded but for two companies, with the majority of the men returning to their original units. The two companies were placed under the overall command of Captain Commandant Thomas Posey, with his subordinates being Captain James Parr, whose company was composed of men mainly

A British Twenty-Fourth Regiment of Foot Sergeants' Fusil, circa 1770. The sergeant's gun was recovered by the Americans at Saratoga. *Courtesy of the James Mitchell Varnum Museum.*

from Pennsylvania, and Captain Gabriel Long, who commanded the remaining Virginians of the old rifle corps.

Posey was born on the family farm adjacent to Mount Vernon. He had shown his fortitude by his command of the pickets during the harsh winter of 1776, with the guards encountering skirmishes as they patrolled on an almost daily basis.

On July 18, Washington sent orders that the Rifle Corps and the Fourth Pennsylvania under command of Lieutenant Colonel William Butler march to Ulster County, New York, and "cooperate with the Militia and to check the Indians if possible." Nearly one year after Governor George Clinton's appeal for help against the raids from indigenous tribes allied with the British, the destruction of frontier homes and property continued nearly unabated. Washington sent $2,500 in advance to Posey for the salaries of his officers and men.

On July 28 in Albany, a return of the rifle corps was made for a total of 109 riflemen, with 55 from Parr's company and 54 from Long's. In Albany, 98 of the men were present and fit for duty.[127]

During the few days they spent in Albany, the men of the rifle corps had their guns repaired and attempted to gather what clothing they could for the march. Lieutenant Colonel Butler complained that "[t]he Rifle men have hardly a Shoe" and that for his own men he "could not be supplied with a single article." Despite this setback, the men readied for the march. The rifle corps and the Fourth Pennsylvania set out on July 30 and reached Schoharie, New York, the following day.

Lieutenant Colonel Butler took command of Fort Defiance, where Loyalists and indigenous raiders had been waging a skulking war for months. Butler was well liked by Washington. In his letter of introduction to the lieutenant colonel's superior, General John Stark, he had praised Butler as an "enterprising good Officer, and well acquainted with the savage mode of warfare." He asked that Butler be placed in command of the frontier troops, as he placed "a great dependence on Colo. Butler's abilities as a Woodsman."[128]

Once at Fort Defiance, Butler intended to take aggressive action against the marauders. He sent out a small, subaltern party to seek out and apprehend one Christopher Service, who lived nearby the Charlotte River and had long been suspected of ferrying supplies to the British. When confronted, Service swung an axe at the men and was shot dead. The party took four other prisoners and set to return.

Word of the American party had reached the neighboring Loyalists, and in short order, a band under command of Captain Charles Smith was headed to rescue the captives.

Lieutenant Colonel Butler received word of the Loyalists' movements and recorded in his journal, "I received intelligence from Genl. Stark of one Smith who had raised a number of Tories and was Marching to Join the Enemy. I immediately detached Capt. Long of the Rifle Corps with a party to intercept their march."

LONG AND HIS MEN crept along the east side of the Schoharie River until discovering Smith and his men on the opposite bank, about fifteen to twenty miles above Upper Fort, the northernmost blockhouse and stockade in the Schoharie Valley. The men sat in wait until a party of the enemy, including Smith, stepped into open ground. According to accounts, Long himself fired and shot the Tory captain through the head. Others fired with that first barrage and "wounded a number." Butler wrote, "A creek unluckily being between the parties when they Engaged prevented Capt. Long from advancing and gave the rest an Opportunity to escape."[129]

Butler's men spent much of the next few months scouting and skirmishing in mostly a defensive posture, a frustrating turn of events for the colonel, who had planned an offensive excursion against the indigenous allies of the British. He would complain to General Clinton that "the little dependence that can be put in the few [local] militia that do turn out, the disaffection of most of the inhabitants to us, the distance and the Wilderness of Country that we have to pass thro to the Enemy without the Necessaries for such an expedition, make it difficult in my present situation to act otherwise."[130]

It was not until October that an offensive was finally manned and marched from the fort for a two-week expedition. A total of 203 men—made up of 122 men of the Fourth Pennsylvania, 56 from the rifle corps, 18 rangers from Lieutenant Dietz's Company and 7 militiamen with five packhorses—set out in the campaign for Onoquaga and Unadilla.

It was an inauspicious beginning. They reached the headwaters of the Delaware River a day later after marching through downpours and along muddy roads for much of the previous day. The men followed the river for two days before heading across the adjacent mountains to reach the Susquehanna River. By October 6, they were just eight miles from Unadilla.

Scouts were sent out to reconnoiter the area and took some prisoners. From them, Butler learned that the enemy had left for Onoquaga just days before. A small party was sent out to capture a man named Glasford, a Tory who would prove useful as a guide, and on October 8, under cover of darkness, the Americans waded through a crossing point on the Susquehanna to reach the settlement. Fearful of an ambush while crossing the river, Colonel Butler had the riflemen lead the crossing and then file off to the left and right as the remainder of the "musketry with fixed bayonets" took the center as they reached the opposite bank. The town, consisting of some forty well-framed houses, was taken largely without incident, and the men "fared sumptuously" on the poultry, vegetables and other provisions left behind. Should the enemy return, the troops built multiple campfires to delude any scouts into believing their numbers were larger than suspected.

The next morning, the men of the Fourth Pennsylvania crossed over, with the mission to collect cattle and corn and, in turn, burn ten houses. The town was just one of several the Americans would plunder in a time-honored albeit unsettling tradition of dividing the bounty (spoils of war) among the troops. The Continental Congress would express concern that such activities might result in the bullying and robbing of innocent individuals, but there was no action taken beyond the recording of that concern on paper.

One solider was shot, reportedly by a Native American, after he stumbled into the woods unarmed, chasing a stray packhorse. In response, Colonel Butler sent Captain Parr and his company about three miles downriver to destroy an Indian village spied by reconnoitering scouts. After Parr's successful mission, his company returned to Onoquaga and took part in burning the village and crops before leaving behind the smoldering ruins in the midafternoon.

The troops re-crossed the river and burned every dwelling they encountered as they began their march to Unadilla. Another downpour on October 10 brought the surrounding creeks and rivers to rise to dangerous levels. Trees were felled to bridge swollen brooks, and horses were compelled to swim across creeks that had been waded through days before. In attempting to cross the Susquehanna, the men were mounted on horseback, sending the beasts wading or swimming back and forth across the river some twenty times.

The raging Delaware proved too intimidating for the troops, and they cut a path through the wilderness to begin the return march to Fort Defiance. The men got briefly lost, but on finding their way, they continued without provisions but for some parched corn procured from a field in passing; they reached their destination on October 16. It was not until after their return that the troops learned of the British attacks on communities far downriver from where they had been searching.

Although the campaign was considered a success by Butler, he soon heard rumors from Oneida scouts aligned with the Americans of a retaliatory raid by Indians aligned with the enemy. He sent the rifle corps to the Upper Fort in the Schoharie Valley. The fort was considered to be the best constructed of the three forts in the valley, strengthened by its "crib work" of parallel walls of logs set horizontally, with its crevices then filled with dirt.

Butler had also sent out scouting parties to learn of the enemy's approach, but there was a surprise attack at Cherry Valley, where some 250 Continental soldiers under command of Colonel Ichabod Alden had taken a lackluster approach to the warnings and were, as a consequence, deprived of many men, the commander being among those killed on November 11.

Although Washington was reportedly pleased with Butler's expedition to destroy the settlements at Onoquaga and Unadilla, he knew that supplies could not be depended on for another, and indeed, although he had ordered some "80 suits of uniform," including shoes and stockings, as well as fifty blankets for the riflemen, he saw delay after delay in their arrival. Even by the New Year, he was unsure that what he had ordered for the men had arrived.

Furthermore, the commander-in-chief needed men for the confrontation with the British in New York, and more musket men were needed there than marksmen. As he had before, he ordered the disbandment of the rifle corps, ordering Major Posey to return to his company on December 20. He wrote to General Clinton of his desire to disband the corps, but left the door open for the general to keep them in New York if their services were still needed. Clinton affirmed his need for them, and Washington deferred. Supplies had still not arrived, and there was little sense in marching a company of poorly clothed men even farther from the provisions still waiting to be shipped from Albany.

Captain Parr was elevated to major to replace Major Posey, and Lieutenant Michael Simpson was promoted to replace Parr. Captain Gabriel Long resigned his commission on May 13, 1799, and was replaced by Captain Lieutenant Philip Slaughter. Although there were plans to have the men march to Wyoming Valley in Pennsylvania should their full clothing arrive, these were never followed through, and the rifle corps remained in the Schoharie Valley for the winter.

By March, the rifle corps held 120 men, of whom 107 were present at the fort and fit for duty. On April 6, 1779, a company of the riflemen under command of Lieutenant Elijah Evans was dispatched, along with a company from the Fourth Pennsylvania, to Cobleskill, New York. There they were joined by the Fifth New York under Captain Johnson, commander of the Lower Fort in the valley. The three companies then marched to Canajoharie and eventually on to Fort Schuyler in Rome, New York.

These men would be among the 588 troops who marched on April 19, 1779, on a five-day, 180-mile excursion against the Onondaga Nation. The resultant sacking and pillage of three Indian villages came on April 21 after word came that an advance scouting party of a company from the First New York had killed one squaw and captured another, along with "two or three children and one White man."[131]

Receiving this word, the remainder of the troops "hurried on with all dispatch in an attempt to take as many prisoners from the three towns which largely comprised the Onondaga population."[132] After a brief skirmish, the towns were abandoned and left to the troops, who gathered some one hundred guns among the plunder and then burned some fifty houses. Among

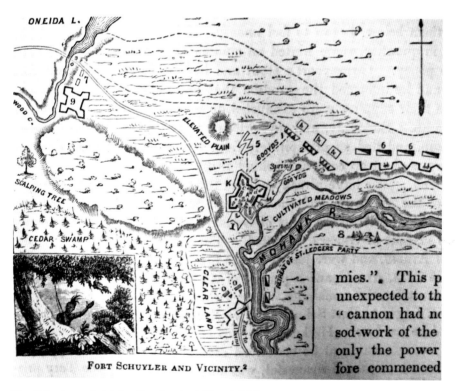

mies.". This p
unexpected to th
"cannon had n
sod-work of the
only the power
fore commenced

Fort Schuyler and vicinity. *From* Lossing's Pictorial History of the Revolutionary War.

the twelve Onondaga killed was "a Negroe who was their Dr." Thirty-four were taken prisoner and marched back to Fort Schuyler.

As many of the Onondaga villagers had fled into the woods, the riflemen were placed in advance to fend off any counterattacks from skulking warriors, as was common in indigenous battles. They met such a party waiting for them across Onondaga Creek, but the accuracy of the riflemen dispersed them quickly back into the woods.

The American troops and their prisoners reached the fort around noon on April 24 with much fanfare. Washington would hail the success of the raids, but it was to be a prelude to a bloody summer, one whose merit is still questioned by historians today.

The remainder of that spring was spent in scouting the surrounding areas of the three forts in the Schoharie Valley in preparation for the much-anticipated assault on the indigenous allies of the British in the Mohawk Valley.

In June 1779, the Fourth Pennsylvania and 120 riflemen assembled at Middle Fort. On the morning of September 11, the company marched from the fort under command of Lieutenant Erkuries Beatty within six days, despite slogging through rain, crossing the Mohawk River and marching through muddied roads to Canajoharie. Once there, they rendezvoused with the Third New York Regiment under Colonel Grosvenor.

On June 19, the rifle corps were with those who had marched a rough seventeen miles to destroy the village of Springfield, only to arrive and find it already destroyed. One the twenty-first, Major Parr was dispatched with one hundred men of the rifle corps and sent on a three-day mission to clear a section of the Susquehanna River on which they would float their bateaux.

Parr relayed a report back that the water level of the river was rapidly lowering with the heat of the summer. Scouting downriver, he found a location roughly ten miles from the outlet that was fed by numerous springs and seemed navigable. On hearing Parr's report, General Clinton ordered two companies of the Sixth Massachusetts to erect a dam at this outlet at the southern end of Lake Otsego.

By August 9, the river had risen to a passable level, and the men quickly loaded and carried their bateaux to the water. The rifle corps were sent in advance boats on the west bank of the Susquehanna with orders not to drift out of sight of the others, On August 12, the troops burned a small Scottish settlement and the Tory Glasford's house nearby. They then continued their path of destruction to the Indian villages belonging to the Tuscarora tribe.

Major Parr and one hundred men were dispatched a week later to destroy the Indian town of Ostiningo. The men traveled up the Chenango River and found that the town had already been burned, perhaps the second such incident of a burn and abandonment before their arrival. The next to fall was the village of Owego.

Clinton and Sullivan's forces gathered by August 22, a combined force of some five thousand men. The rifle corps was detached to General Edward Hand's brigade, which comprised the rifle corps, the Fourth Pennsylvania, the light infantry and a handful of volunteers. The rifle corps as such retained a prominent role in the campaign, as ordered: "As there are four cos. of light infantry annexed to Butler's, the Rifle Corps together with other such Rifle Men as may be added to them, are to be a separate corps and kept advanced of the Army as General Hand may direct."[133]

The journal of Lieutenant Beatty of the Fourth Pennsylvania gives us as accurate a description of the expedition as we may find, as well as pertaining to the activities of the rifle corps. On Sunday the twenty-first, he recorded, "Arrived at Tioga 11 oClock where we found Gen. Hand's Brigade encamped one Mile above the mouth of the Tioga where they was building 4 block

Example of a blockhead fort located in Winslow, Maine. *Courtesy of Norman Desmarais.*

houses. The other troops was encamped on the point which was Genl. Poor's & Maxwell's brigades. We encamped on the right of the whole."

By Thursday, around 11:00 a.m., the troops had set out, leaving their heavy baggage and women at the garrison. Packhorses carried provisions for twenty-seven days, and they pulled seven pieces of ordnance and three ammunition wagons as well. Those wagons broke down the following day and delayed their march until 2:00 p.m.

On Sunday morning, however, after marching but three miles, "we found the enemy strongly entrenched with Logs, Dirt, brush &c. The firing imidiately begun in front with the Rifle Corp & the Indians made great halooing. Orders were given then for the troops to form in line of battle which was done. Genl. Hand's brigade in front but none of the troops advanced as we discovered the main body of the enemy was here and had their front secured by a large Morass & brook, their right by the river, & on their left partly in the rear was a very large hill. Their lines extended upward of a mile."[134]

Despite the large force they now faced, the rifle corps led the ensuing battle:

The firing was kept up very briskly by the Rifle men & a company who was sent to reinforce them. Likewise the Indians returned the fire very brisk with many shouts for about 2 hours while a disposition was made for to attack them. Genl. Clinton & Poor's Brigades was sent off round their left flank to take possession of the hill in the enemy's rear and extend their line intirely around them if Possible. After they had gone about half an hour Genl. Hand's brigade advanced in a line of battle with all our artillery in the Centre within about 300 yards of the Enemy's works but in full View of them. A very heavy cannonade began & throwing of Shells.

After another half hour of this intense exchange, "The Enemy retreated up the hill in a great Disorder & as they got near the top received a very heavy fire from Genl. Poor's brigade....As soon as the Enemy left their works, Genl. Hand's brigade pursued them up the hill as far as Genl. Poor was when we made a halt. The riflemen pursued them about one mile farther and made a Negro prisoner, likewise saw some of their wounded going up the river in Canoes."

The troops continued upriver the following day, burning more houses and destroying "all the corn in our way." They continued their march on land, and by September 7, they had reached Kandasago, "the Chief town in the

Seneca nation." The town of seventy to eighty houses had been abandoned but for a white child they found wandering the emptied streets. The child's age was guessed to be about three years. He could barely walk and spoke no English. An officer took him into his care, and he was likely among the detachment left behind to "bring our Straggled horses and cattle."

The brigades marched on, seemingly one step behind the enemy as they encountered the still smoldering town of Kanandaqua, and on September 12, they were so close that "we could Discover their tracks very fresh and the water muddy where they had crossed."

The inevitable encounter occurred the following day after reaching the small abandoned town of Adjuste beside a small lake, where they drew provisions and stopped to rest. Fatigue parties were sent out to collect more stores from the ten to fifteen houses they would later burn. Beatty wrote, "About 10 oClock we heard guns firing in front. The troops were immediately formed and marched over the Inlett of the Lake, a very bad morass & Creek and a large hill on the opposite side where we found the Indians who was formed on this hill, had fired on the surveyor & his party & had mortally wounded one of his men. The Rifle Men rushed up the hill & the Enemy made their escape as soon as possible, leaving behind them their Packs, Hats, &c. which the Rifle Men got."

After securing the hill, the brigades learned the fate of Lieutenant Boyd's unfortunate expedition, as described in an earlier chapter. The men recovered "4 or 5 of our men Dead & scalped," but Boyd was not among them. The brigades remained on alert until sunrise, and then at noon on September 14, they marched for a branch of the Jinasee River. Crossing, the men continued through a great expanse of meadows filled with wild grasses as tall as their heads. They crossed the winding Jinasee once again and then another three miles through the woods to reach the town of Chenesee.

Beatty recorded, "On entering the town we found the body of Lt. Boyd and another Rifle Man in a most terrible mangled condition." Both men had been beheaded and their bodies mutilated in multiple ways. The soldiers were immediately buried with honors, and nearly the entirety of the following day from reveille at 6:00 a.m. until well after nightfall was spent in destroying crops and corn.

"Some of it we husked and threw in the River," the Lieutenant wrote, "the rest we Carried to the houses & burned. The whole we totally destroyed. After 10 oClock we received orders to begin our march home which we did, leaving the town in flames."

Upon their return to Tioga on the twenty-fifth, a celebratory feast was ordered, with General Sullivan ordering that each brigade be given "one of the best oxen there was & 5 gallons of Spirits." That night, the officers gathered under the canopy of a large bower illuminated by thirteen pine knot fires and drank thirteen toasts to Lieutenant Boyd and the riflemen who had been lost in the expedition.

Washington formally praised the efforts of Sullivan's forces against the indigenous allies of the enemy in his general orders on October 17: "[T]heir whole country has been overrun and laid waste." Indeed, forty towns and their surrounding fields had been destroyed. Fewer than forty Americans had been killed in the encounters with indigenous warriors. The loss of Native Americans is estimated to have been larger in the battles, and with the destruction of crops, many more would die of starvation during the following winter.

Despite the heavy losses, some indigenous warriors fled to British-held Niagara, and as time would prove, despite being humbled, it was not the end of the Iroquois Confederacy's role in the Revolutionary War.

THE ROLE OF THE riflemen during the American Revolution forever changed military strategy on both sides of the Atlantic. The formation of rifle corps in the United States and in Great Britain continued after the war. The guerrilla tactics used so successfully by the corps were incorporated worldwide and are still studied and practiced in the twenty-first century.

Chapter 6

THE MEN OF MARBLEHEAD

Any introduction to the reader of those fishermen and dockworkers from the Cape Cod town of Marblehead, Massachusetts, would not do justice to the words of Frank A. Gardner, MD, their first biographer, who wrote, "Few regiments in the entire Continental Army were in more important engagements, or rendered greater service."[135]

Incorporating a militia unit on January 10, 1775, the town made provisions "to pay persons who may enlist as minutemen, and take other suitable steps for perfecting the militia in the arts of war." Then £800 was granted and a committee of three assigned to oversee the distribution of funds by James Mugford, the appointed paymaster, at the following rates: "2 shillings a day to a private, 3 shillings to sergeants, clerks, drummers and fifers, 4 shillings to second lieutenants, 8 pence to first lieutenants, and six shillings a day to captains."

The men of Marblehead would become best known for the handful of them represented in the 1850 painting *Washington Crossing the Delaware* by German American immigrant Emanuel Leutze. It is those men of Marblehead around Washington, scanning the river ahead, breaking up the ice before the bow and rowing through the prevailing blizzard. The painting depicts just one episode of many that displayed their navigational skills, hardiness and grit—as stealthy as the riflemen on water—as well as their adaptability to fight on both sea and land, all of which would place them in a distinction of their own.

Detail from *Washington Crossing the Delaware River* (1851) by Emanuel Leutze, as printed in *American Heritage Magazine. Courtesy of the Smithsonian Institute.*

Although the unit was organized primarily as a marine unit, its history includes important contributions to some of the most important land engagements of the war, as Gardner alluded. Captain John Glover was appointed colonel of the Marblehead militia. Glover was a wealthy member of the "codfish aristocracy," which dominated the commerce of the North Atlantic coast. The crews aboard his sloops and schooners had long suffered harassment by the British from both corrupt customs officers and illegal impressments by British warships on the high seas. Although he had prospered in the British colonies, these infringements turned him against the empire.[136]

The militia soon received a cargo of weapons, which were distributed to enlistees about town. Recruitment was soon boosted by an event that was one of the earliest confrontations of the war—and a prelude to the events at Concord and Lexington.

On Sunday, February 26, 1775, the 240 men of the Sixty-Fourth Regiment under British lieutenant colonel Alexander Leslie landed at Marblehead during the hour of worship to avoid detection, with instructions to march ahead to Salem and seize nineteen French cannons known to British intelligence to have been purchased by David Mason of the town.

The British-appointed Governor Thomas Gage knew that the men of Salem were arming themselves, and being a wealthy and international seaport, it was perhaps not surprising that a patriotic merchant would support the cause with foreign-made weaponry. It is unknown, however, whether Gage also knew that the cannons had already been mounted on carriages by blacksmith and militia captain Robert Foster, in whose shop the guns lay hidden on the north side of the North River.

The troops marched along the Bay Road from Marblehead, reportedly playing "Yankee Doodle Dandy" to mock the villagers. But a warning from Marblehead had reached Salem before the redcoats arrived. Upon reaching the bridge at the southern entrance of the town, they found planks already torn up from the bridge and the bells in the steeples of the town ringing loudly to alert the citizens. Undaunted, the British regulars fixed bayonets and loaded their muskets, and once the bridge was repaired, they marched into the public square under martial music with colors flying. They attracted the attention of at least one Tory sympathizer, who told them where the cannons were confined, and Leslie soon guided his troops toward the North Bridge.

Mason, who was also a colonel in the Salem militia, sounded the alarm in the North Church and then rode to Foster's shop to protect the cannons. When he arrived, actions had already been taken to impede the British from seizing the munitions. Men under the Salem militia's commander, Timothy Pickering, had rushed to the river and raised the drawbridge The British commander demanded that the townspeople gathered lower the bridge, to no avail; in fact, some of those gathered climbed to the top of the upended leaf to mock the soldiers standing helpless at attention on the other side.

Leslie refused to withdraw and swore that he would cross the bridge no matter the consequences or loss of men to do so. While he stood his ground, the alarm had been sounded in surrounding towns, and an estimated ten thousand minutemen were forming and gathering toward the town. Still, Lieutenant Colonel Leslie stewed, declaring that it was the Kings Road and that he should cross before he returned to Boston. It was, in fact, a road built by the owners of the lots on each side of the river and under no jurisdiction but their own.

Gardner's history tells of a minuteman named Symonds who stood guard at the top of the bridge all during the standoff. At one point, Leslie had

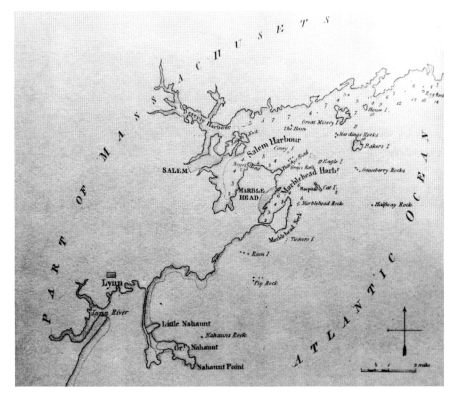

Early map of Salem and Marblehead. *Courtesy of Wikimedia Commons.*

reportedly given the order for his soldiers to fire on the civilians gathered, but it was not carried out, perhaps due to the efforts of Captain John Felt of the Salem militia, who persuaded him to negotiate a peaceful end to the confrontation.

Leslie eventually agreed that if the drawbridge were lowered, he would march his men, without inflicting any harm, about fifty rods beyond the bridge and then turnabout. The British commander was instructed to tell Gage that he had crossed the bridge into town but found no guns.

This was accomplished peacefully, and the humiliated British retreated to Marblehead. Unbeknownst to them, legions of minutemen lined the road to Homan's Cove, where the British vessel lay at low tide. Word had reached them, however, that violence had, for the time, been avoided; orders were given to let the redcoats pass unmolested.

This small but significant incident was an auspicious beginning for the men of Marblehead. It was widely reported and published in a popular pamphlet as "Leslie's Retreat." The victory emboldened the seaside communities along the Cape. By late May, after the similar standoffs in Lexington and Concord, the fifers and drummers parading and calling for fishermen to enlist in the Continental army were doing a brisk business.

On May 30, Glover turned out the regiment on an alarm that the British were landing at the ferry. It proved false, but this was an indication that preparedness had finally been achieved for the town. On June 10, Glover received an order from the Provincial Committee of Safety to "continue the Regiment under his command at Marblehead, until further orders, and to hold them in readiness to march at a moment's warning to any post where he may be directed."

By this time, Glover had composed ten companies from his enlistees, some 405 men, including officers, from the towns of Marblehead, Beverly, Salem and Lynn, Massachusetts. A report sent to Congress indicated that "about three-quarters of said number are armed with effective fire-locks, who are willing and chosen to serve in the army under him, all now at Marblehead."[137]

The Provincial Committee recommended that four men be commissioned chief colonels in the army and that other officers be duly assigned "as soon as the list of them can be settled." Colonel Glover was officially commissioned on June 16, 1775, and placed in command of the Twenty-First Regiment of Massachusetts. The regiment received orders to march on the twenty-first, reached Cambridge the following day and joined the Provincial Army under General Ward.

The men of the regiment, in their "blue round jacket and trousers trimmed with leather buttons," made a favorable impression on Washington and his officers, as did Glover himself, noted to be "the most finely dressed officer of the army at Cambridge."[138]

Captain Alexander Graydon of Pennsylvania recalled in his memoir of the war years that "there was an appearance of discipline in this corps; the officers seemed to have mixed with the world, and to understand what belonged to their stations." Graydon also noted that there were black mariners among the men from Marblehead, "which to persons unaccustomed to such associations, had a disagreeable, degrading effect." As with Washington, many officers were uneasy with the regiments that included men of color. As Glover's men were mostly from the vessels that plied the sea, their longstanding social customs as shipmates often differed from those accustomed to the laws and prejudices on land.

The colonel made a most favorable impression on Washington, especially when he learned firsthand of his own devised plans for capturing some of the British supply ships en route to Boston Harbor. As Gardner wrote in his biography of the regiment, "The fact that the organization contained so many seafaring men made it unique as a military body, and at this period, as well as several times later in its career, this circumstance greatly increased its utility. Colonel Glover early foresaw what might be accomplished on the water."

Having several vessels already at his disposal, Glover laid out a plan for outfitting these and other vessels for privateering, their immediate mission being to halt the constant flow of British supply ships entering Boston Harbor.

Washington approved these plans, and volunteers were coming to Cambridge by August. Their first venture, sailing from Beverly, Massachusetts, on September 5 in the schooner *Hannah*, resulted in the capture of the British ship *Unity*, laden with provisions and munitions.[139]

By October, the general had sent Glover, his regiment and volunteers to be stationed in Beverly for the express purpose of assembling, outfitting and manning a fleet of privateering vessels. Within three months, ten prizes lay at anchor in the harbor.

Such success was certain to attract attention and retaliation from the British, and Colonel Glover was given the task of completing fortifications around the port. The first fortification was completed in February 1776 on a peninsula known as Tuck's Point, which historian George Athan Billias described as "an arm of land…which jutted out to sea just in front of the wharves that lined Beverly's shore. Built as a sandbank battery and laid out in five embrasures, the fort was armed with two six-pound fieldpieces. Probably because of Glover's influence, cannon for the fort were obtained on loan from Marblehead."[140]

Work on expanding the fortifications continued through spring, with the Committee of Safety requesting that Glover's Brigade "[b]uild sum Brest Works at West Beach and other Places in the Town." By the beginning of summer, five more of these sandbank batteries had been erected at strategic locations to protect the harbor.

During the months that these defenses were being built, Glover had also focused on training the recruits from January 1776 for his brigade, which was now designated the Fourteenth Continental of Massachusetts. As these men were to man the fortifications, he set a strict routine in camp, from spit and polish inspections to bayonet training and awarding new guns, ammunition and pouches to men who excelled in their learning the arts of war.

He built extensive barracks for the troops at what would later be known as Queen's Park, rented quarters for others nearby and saw that the men would be fed well, even sending hot meals to the guards at isolated posts around the harbor.

Glover was given little time to rest on any laurels. Just as the fortifications had been finished, he was called up with a contingent of men to march to New York for what was seen as the battle for Manhattan.

The regiment arrived on August 9 and was assigned to General John Sullivan's Brigade. Within days, men of the regiment had outfitted a pair of fireboats and attempted to fire two British vessels anchored near Tarrytown. The regiment remained stationed on New York Island, and while not engaged in the fighting of the Battle of Long Island on August 27, the men were to play a vital role in saving the American army in defeat, for the victories that lay ahead.

At five o'clock in the morning, Glover and his regiment were ferried as reinforcements to a position on a small peninsula of the East River between Fort Putnam and Wallabout Bay. The fort soon became the focus of the British attack, and Glover's regiment engaged the approaching enemy throughout its first night. Despite its efforts, by the morning of the twenty-ninth the British were digging trenches just a few thousand feet from the fort.

The day brought a drenching storm, as well as wind that prevented the British warships from moving up the East River. It bought the Americans time, and Washington took advantage to organize a retreat off Long Island.

The army had just ten flat-bottomed boats to transport troops, so his first orders were to General Heath stationed at Kings Bridge, and his quartermaster, to confiscate any suitable watercraft, especially such flat-bottomed boats, which could carry horses and equipment as well as the men. Regiments were placed on alert and told to be ready to move at a moment's notice, although none knew that meant a nighttime evacuation.

As George Athan Billias noted, "The success or failure of the evacuation now rested solely upon those manning the craft. Washington entrusted the fate of his entire force to two regiments drawn from Essex County, Massachusetts. One was Glover's Fourteenth; the other was Israel Hutchinson's Twenty-Seventh, a unit made up largely from fishermen and sailors hailing from Salem, Lynn, and Danvers. These Massachusetts mariners were pitting their seamen's skills against three factors that might make a shambles of the operation—time, tide, and wind."[141]

At about 10:00 p.m., Glover's regiment slipped away from its position to rendezvous with Hutchinson's mariners at the site of the Brooklyn Ferry. A contingent of craft from sailing vessels to rowboats had been procured.

Under cover of darkness, the experienced seamen began to navigate across the river. At first the ebb tide and a strong northeast wind made the passage difficult, but when the wind changed direction to the southwest and a fog settled in the early hours of the morning, the men were able to successfully transport some nine thousand troops, as well as horses and equipment, to safety in about nine hours.

The performance of Glover's regiment in the Long Island operations made a strong impression on Washington. He put the men from Marblehead to work on the waterways, establishing two boat stations on the East and North Rivers and ordering that military supplies be transported by water whenever land transport could not be spared or roads became impassable.

Washington planned to rely on Glover's regiment when he fashioned a plan to evacuate the remainder of his forces as well as military supplies from the city to the north and the Jersey shore. He petitioned the State of New York for four schooners from Albany and made due preparations. By September 12, however, the vessels had still not arrived, and two days later, Glover was ordered to rejoin the army at Harlem: "[L]eaving their tents and baggage at the bank of the river to be transported up the Hudson, the brigade marched to the north. That was the last Glover's men ever saw of their equipment." The planned evacuation of the sick and wounded did not occur until the British began their invasion of Manhattan at about noon on September 15.[142]

Howe's amphibious landing at Kip's Bay, between Harlem and the city, overwhelmed the American fortifications there. Manned by the Connecticut militia, the flimsy fortifications were soon leveled under the intense shelling from British warships in the harbor. So intense was the shelling that two regiments sent to reinforce the men at the shoreline turned and joined them in retreat.

Washington, riding into the scene of battle, tried to rally the men into taking a defensive stand, but these same troops panicked when the first British landing party came into view. Dr. Morgan was also witness to this scene and wrote in his journal:

> At the approach of an advanced party of British troops, after landing at York Island, about three hundred of the men, who were advantageously stationed for opposing them, retreated, without giving fire, with great precipitation; or in common language, ran away. They were met by Glover's regiment, which stopped their flight….The officers of Colonel Glover's regiment, one of the best corps in the service…immediately obliged the fugitive officers

and soldiers equally, to turn into the ranks with the soldiers of Glover's
regiment…to march back to the ground they had quitted.[143]

One man left behind in the evacuation was Captain Nathan Hale. The young Yale-educated schoolteacher from East Haddam, Connecticut, had volunteered for a reconnaissance mission to determine the British forces' next move. Although he had little experience with such missions and was, in the view of his close friend, "too frank and open for deceit and disguise,"[144] Hale yearned to contribute to the cause of independence in a meaningful and memorable way. On September 13, Hale exchanged his army uniform for the plain brown garb and broad-brimmed hat of a schoolmaster, and taking his diploma with him as proof of his occupation, he was ferried from Norwalk, Connecticut, to a landing place near Hutchinson, Long Island.

Once there, however, Hale found that most of the British forces had left to take part in the assault on Manhattan. He decided to follow the redcoats across the East River, arriving on the island in time to see the British setting up tents in the encampments the Americans had abandoned and constructing earthworks to defend their new positions. He also noticed American deserters arriving at the encampments, and this may have caused him to abandon his mission after drawing a few sketches and taking notes, which he folded up and placed in his shoe before heading back to Long Island and the rendezvous that would bring him safely back to the American lines.

On September 21, he was still a day's walk away from the appointed meeting place with Captain Pond, near Flushing, New York. While there, he was recognized in a tavern by the notorious Robert Rogers. The American major had earned a reputation for ruthlessness during the French and Indian War, when rangers under his command conducted brutal raids throughout New England. Rogers had fled persecution for debt after the war and ended up in jail there under similar circumstances. He had reappeared in America in 1775, playing a wily game with Washington and others, professing loyalty to the American cause but arousing their suspicions almost at once. In July 1776, he had been placed under guard by the Americans in Philadelphia, although he soon made his escape to a British ship in the harbor.

Historical speculation has it that Rogers recognized Hale and arranged a meeting with him at the tavern, where the young schoolmaster's gullibility was taken advantage of by Rogers's professions of loyalty to the American cause. Hale had, in fact, revealed the true nature of his mission to the eager Loyalist, and when he showed for a meeting with Rogers and what he believed were American sympathizers, he was immediately seized as a spy.

Hale was taken to General Howe and interrogated at Beekman House, the large estate the British had confiscated as headquarters, and imprisoned overnight in a greenhouse on the property. Facing his impending execution, the young captain requested a Bible and a visit from a clergyman. Both were denied the prisoner.

On the Sabbath morning of September 22, Hale was marched down the Post Road to the Park of Artillery, located adjacent to the Dove Tavern, now at the intersection of Sixty-Sixth and Third Streets, where he was hanged before a small but attentive crowd of British officers and onlookers.

His final moments were remarked on by several witnesses, who marveled at the composure of the young officer, and the words he uttered to those gathered were recorded and later recounted by British captain John Montresor. Hale defended his mission and told the audience that he "thought it the duty of every good Officer to obey any orders given by his Commander-in-Chief," and he warned those witnesses to "be at all times prepared to meet death in whatever shape it might appear." The young schoolteacher's last words echoed those of Cato, a rebel against Caesar's tyranny in Rome, with Hale exclaiming his regret "that I have but one life to lose for my country."[145]

THE HISTORIAN BILLIAS POINTS to the rarely mentioned Battle of Pelham Bay as an action that highlighted Glover's skills as a military tactician and commander, whether on land or sea.

Skirmishes continued around the island through mid-September. It was widely anticipated that General Howe would attempt another amphibious landing before the onset of winter, and on October 15, the British general launched a large-scale assault on Westchester County. The British warships "sailed in a wide sweep northeast by way of Hell's Gate and the East River, up into Long Island Sound."[146]

Howe's troops landed on Throggs Neck, behind the American lines. Washington immediately sent reinforcements to key locations along the Sound where other enemy troops might make a landing. Glover was placed in charge of the remnants of four Massachusetts regiments: Glover's own Fourteenth, with 179 men; the Thirteenth, with 226 men; the Third Massachusetts, with 204 men; and the Twenty-Sixth, holding 234 soldiers, totaling 843 men.

On the morning of October 18, Glover wrote to a friend in New Hampshire, "I went on the hill with my glass and discovered a number of ships in the Sound underway, the small boats, upwards of two hundred, all manned and filled with troops."

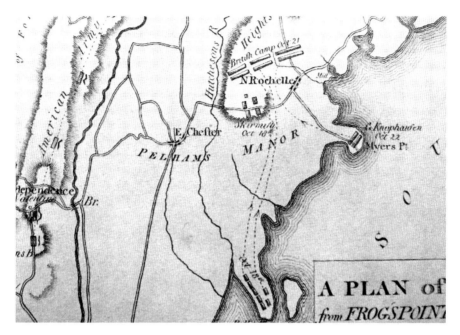

Detail of a map of Pelham Bay. *Courtesy of Wikimedia Commons.*

Glover would leave the Fourteenth with three cannons on the high bank on the west side of the Hutchinson river to guard the rear of his march to Pelham Bay, leaving him a force of 750 men to face the British.

Glover formed his men and began a quick march to Pelham, positioning his troops behind the stone walls on both sides of the road leading into town from Pell's Point. The colonel also sent a skirmishing party of forty men to slow the British approach. Glover's men met the approaching landing party head on and the first volley from the British had little effect, but the return fire of Glover's men quickly brought four of the enemy down. The exchange of fire continued, and when the American party withdrew, after losing two men and several wounded, the British troops triumphantly marched on, unaware of the American ambush that lay ahead.

When the redcoats reached the position of Colonel Read's regiment of 200 men, the more than 1,100 British troops were met with heavy fire from a diverse contingent of weaponry, including muskets, fowling guns and long rifles.

The American volley caused the immediate retreat of the forward troops to the rear, where the main army was located. Read's men hunkered down behind the walls for another attack. When the British responded an hour and a half later, four thousand British regulars and as many as two hundred Hessians, covered by the shelling from seven cannons, advanced down the narrow winding road that locals called Wolf's Lane.

The cannonade had little effect on the men behind the stone walls, who knew instinctively that it would cease once the troops had advanced close to their position. When the British column came within thirty feet of Read's position, the Americans again fired a volley of lead into the road. It halted the British advance momentarily, but their fire was quickly returned, as Glover would write, "with showers of musketry and cannonballs."

Read's men held the British advance on the road for another twenty minutes before retreating under cover of stone walls and brush to the junction of Wolf's Lane with Split Rock Road, and shortly after, they joined the regiment under Shephard at his position. The combined force fired on the British again at their approach, and another intense exchange of gunfire followed. The American units fired a total of seventeen rounds at the enemy, and the British responded with a continual rain of fire for more than an hour.

The British artillery soon had brought up its cannons, and when it was discovered that the enemy troops were attempting to outflank the Americans, Colonel Glover ordered a retreat. The remainder of the three regiments backtracked and waded through the Hutchinson River under cover of the three cannons and gunfire from the Fourteenth Regiment.

Glover wrote, "After fighting all day without victuals or drink, laying as picket all night, the heavens over us and the earth under us, which was all we had having left our baggage at the old encampment we left in the morning."

Outmanned but not out maneuvered, Glover had utilized the New England landscape to his best advantage and shown that even small numbers of men could successfully disrupt the disciplined British tactics of war. Both Washington and General Henry Lee would publicly state in their general orders their appreciation of the courage and fortitude displayed by the men of Marblehead.

In the days that followed, the brigade continued to cover Washington's retreat to White Plains, New York. The brigade also undertook an excursion to retrieve two hundred barrels of flour and pork left behind at Eastchester. Again setting out under cover of darkness, Glover and his men recovered and returned the goods without the notice of British lookouts.

Members of the brigade were also sent out as scouting parties, and in one skirmish with a party of Hessians, they killed twelve of the German soldiers and took another three prisoner, including a mounted officer whose horse was ridden as a trophy back to camp.[147]

Such operations would prove to give Washington ample time to get his troops to safety and, especially, to help the rear guard, which struggled to move baggage, artillery and military goods up to the main army. While Washington had reached the village of White Plains on October 22, Lee's rear guard was in very real danger of being overrun by Howe's troops. Such a disaster nearly came to be on October 25.

Howe's advance guard that day had come within four miles of the village. They were soon spotted by the Americans as the British columns fanned to the left and right of their position. General Lee hurriedly formed his men and began a march to North Castle some fourteen miles to the northeast, a miscalculated attempt to outpace the enemy to the site. Glover recorded that after marching what he estimated to be only about three miles, "We saw the right column advancing on a cross road to cut us off, not more than three quarters of a mile distance."

Lee's division narrowly escaped by turning west onto Dobb's Ferry Road,[148] but as Billias described it, "Only by means of a forced all-night march did Lee's division finally succeed in eluding Howe's columns."[149]

Glover's Brigade would then be stationed at North Castle for the next month until the end of November, when Lee received orders to march the regiments and join Washington in New Jersey. On December 8, General Washington had but 1,700 men. Within a few days, another 3,000 troops with General Sullivan had joined the army and prepared for an assault on the Hessian-held town of Trenton, New Jersey.

Much has been written about that assault on the night of December 25. The account by Billias focuses on those efforts of the men from Marblehead:

> *Christmas night brought with it a howling storm; the first phase of the Battle of Trenton became a struggle against the elements, not the enemy. An angry wind roared down, churning the river waters and making difficult the handling of pitching craft.…The Delaware at the ferrying place was only about 1,000 feet wide, yet Glover's soldiers were forced to call upon all of their seamen's skills to navigate this short span. Great chunks of ice came surging downstream…to smash against the sides of the boats. As they ground to a halt, the huge slabs became obstacles as they clung alongside and impeded the forward progress of the craft. Each cake of ice had to be wrestled out of the way before the boats could continue their progress.*

"The floating ice on the river," wrote Colonel Henry Knox to his wife two days later, "made the labor almost incredible." Knox would make the feat a legend even in his own time, when he addressed Congress as a general near the close of the war:

> *I wish the members of this body knew the people of Marblehead as well as I do—I could wish that they had stood on the banks of the Delaware river in 1776 in that bitter night when the Commander-in-Chief drawn up his little army to cross it, and had seen the powerful current bearing on the floating masses of ice….I wish…that they could have heard the distinguished warrior demand—*Who will lead us on? *and seen the men of Marblehead and Marblehead alone stand forward to lead the army on the perilous path to unfading glories and honors in the achievements of Trenton. There sir, went the fishermen of Marblehead, alike at home upon land or water, alike ardent, patriotic and unflinching, whenever they unfurled the flag of the country.*[150]

Glover and his men left Trenton shortly after the victory that so bolstered the Continental army. Weary of war and with their terms of service set to expire, many longed to return to the sea. Washington was hopeful that he could enlist a fair number aboard the frigates of the Continental navy, but there is little evidence that the men of Glover's Brigade took the general up on that offer, even with the bounty promised by Congress. Many of them likely joined privateering crew, whose members traditionally received a share of the spoils.

Colonel Glover himself remained in Marblehead, although Washington attempted to cajole him back into service with a promotion to brigadier general in January 1777. Glover hesitated to accept the offer. Like many of his men, family and home concerns had grown in their absence. Glover needed to address growing debts, and his wife had fallen ill as well, adding to his reluctance to leave her side.

After considerable delay, the colonel wrote to Washington in April and professed that he did not feel himself worthy of the higher rank. He received in reply an irrefutable epistle of praise from the commander: "I think I may tell you without flattery, that I know of no man better qualified than you to conduct a Brigade. You have activity and industry; and as you know

Sketch of General John Glover, unattributed. *Courtesy of Wikimedia Commons.*

very well the duty of a colonel, you know how to exact that duty from others."[151] Washington closed his letter by urging Glover to return as soon as possible to the brigade that waited for him at Peekskill, New York.

When the brigadier general did arrive in mid-June, he found the remnants of his brigade in a demoralized state. The shortages of supplies over the winter and into spring had left the troops without clothing and equipment needed to resume the campaign for independence. Glover's Brigade now totaled a mere 583 men, with 3 colonels to oversee the regiments. He wrote at once to the Massachusetts Board of War for assistance: "The troops from our State make a most shocking appearance, without shoes, stockings, or breeches....I have seen soldiers go on duty with...nothing to cover their nakedness but a blanket...but I forbear; pray let this matter [be attended to]."[152]

At the end of June, the brigade was ordered back to Eastchester, where it resumed a defensive position of guarding approaches to the north along the Hudson River just a few miles from the British-held Fort Independence. Although his original regiment of seafaring men had long been disbanded, Glover was able to enlist some forty seaworthy men capable of running supplies and handling the craft needed by General George Clinton.

In July, Glover's Brigade was ordered to sail up to Albany and take part in the campaign to stop Burgoyne's drive into the Mohawk Valley. That spring, the British general nicknamed "Gentleman Johnny" for his dashing appearance had taken Ticonderoga without a fight, while a smaller force under Colonel St. Leger marched nearly unimpeded toward Fort Stanwix. A fortress built during the French and Indian War, the fort guarded an invaluable portage place between the main waterway leading to the Mohawk and Hudson Rivers and a waterway to the northwest interior and Lake Ontario.

When Glover's Brigade reached General Schuyler's army outside Saratoga on August 1, the men learned that Burgoyne had marched past the old wooden garrison at Fort Anne, and slowed only by the American troops fleeing Ticonderoga, he was already within striking distance of the town.

It was at Saratoga where the men from Marblehead first engaged the Iroquois warriors who had aligned with Great Britain. Raids from the warriors were perpetrated day and night, and scouting parties were certain to be ambushed. The brief and bloody skirmishes that were preludes to the battles left some twenty-five or thirty Americans dead and just as many taken prisoner.[153]

The brigade was ordered back from Saratoga to Stillwater, a few miles farther from the enemy, with as many stores as it could bring along, including "large droves of cattle, sheep, and hogs." Glover would write in a state of desperation to Jas. Warren in Congress, "Our army at this Post is weak and shattered, much confused, and by no means equal to the enemy; nor is there the least probability of a re-enforcement."

The brigadier general outlined the crisis. On August 6, the day he penned the letter, some two hundred of Colonel Long's New Hampshire regiment were marching home, their terms of service having expired. On the tenth, another five hundred men from Poor's regiment of the county of Hampshire would depart, and two days after, the six hundred men of Nixon's Brigade from the county of Berkshire would leave as well. In the aftermath of these departures, the post would have but three thousand men to face Burgoyne's combined forces, "who from the best accounts we can collect are at least 8,000, and every day growing stronger, by the disaffected inhabitants joining them, and ours growing weaker."[154]

Reinforcements would eventually arrive later in the month, along with General Gates, who would take command of the northern army. While General Schuyler had troops engaged in precautionary measures, diverting streams, rolling heavy stones onto the roadway and felling trees across the same route the British would have to take, Gates took a more aggressive approach. On September 8, less than a month after taking command, he ordered the troops to advance for the first time in months some thirteen miles to Bemis Heights above the Hudson River. There, working with Polish engineer Thaddeus Kosciusko, the soldiers worked feverishly erecting batteries and breastworks within the natural obstacles of stone walls, thick woods and rugged terrain.

Glover's Brigade was situated on the heights above one of the narrowest stretches of the river, with the mission of manning the fortifications they had erected to the right of the Fort Neilson redoubt, located on the crest of Bemis Heights. With the brigade now reinforced by four regiments of Massachusetts's regulars and another three regiments from New York, the men prepared for what would become known as the Battles of Saratoga.

On September 13, Burgoyne moved his troops to the west bank of the Hudson. It was a march of no return, yet he was confident that he would be victorious against Gates's prepared defenses. He personally led the attack on September 19 near Freeman's Farm, which tore into the left wing of the American defenses. During this engagement, Glover's along with Nixon's and most of Paterson's Brigades remained posted at the works in front of their encampment, waiting for any order to march as reinforcements.

The call came for reinforcements to the right flank, but no records indicate that Glover's men entered into battle that day. In the wake of that first battle, Glover dispatched his men on the ever-effective raiding parties that his brigade had specialized in on land. On the twenty-seventh, Glover led a group of one hundred men "to take off a picquet of about 60 of the enemy, who were posted about half a mile from me; at the same time ordered a covering party of 200 to support them. This being the first enterprise of this kind and as it was proposed by me, I was anxious for its success."[155]

General Gates also put troops to work strengthening those fortifications that had already been laid. Glover wrote that "we are making every preparation to receive them, by felling trees and abetting the passes between North River and Saratoga Lake."

Six miles lay between the two bodies of water. Troops around this time were also shifted as well, with Glover's Brigade being sent east on September 22 to the lower works along the river, close by the Bemis Tavern and the pontoon bridge that Gates had built across the Hudson.

Gates waited in anticipation. He had guessed that the British general would "endeavor by one rash stroke to regain all they have lost." That effort came on October 7, when Burgoyne led a force of some 1,500 British and German regulars along with a detachment of Canadians and indigenous warriors against the left wing of the American army.[156]

But British reconnaissance efforts had provided the general with limited information. When he had to pause and confer with officers after little more than a mile, Gates took the opportunity to send Morgan's riflemen to attack the redcoats' right flank and followed that by sending Poor's regiment and Learned's Brigade to cover the center and left flanks in a three-pronged attack.

Glover's Brigade again stood ready at its post. While some early historians placed the brigadier general in the thick of the battle, even at Benedict Arnold's side as he rallied a charge on a redoubt, Billias in his biography uncovered evidence that shows that the regiment was not called on until late in the fray. Sergeant Ebenezer Wild recorded the movements of the brigade that day:

> *This afternoon about 3 o'clk we were alarmed. We marched out as far as our advanced picket; stayed there till about sunset. About 5 o'clk an engagement began on our left wing which lasted until sunset,—very brisk on both sides. About sunset our Bd Major brought us the news that we gained the ground on the enemy's right wing and made a great sloter of*

them—taken a great number of prisoners with considerable booty. Our brigade marched off from our lines in order to attack their lines upon their left; but it being pretty dark, and not to our advantage to attack them at that time of night, we returned to our camps again.

If the members of the brigade were disappointed that, yet again, they had been left out of contributing to a major battle, their actions a few days later would save the army from unmitigated disaster.

Burgoyne had moved his men into a strong position on the heights of Saratoga, just north of the mouth of the Fishkill River. On these heights, he mounted twenty-seven cannons that overlooked the river and the farmlands of the Argyle Valley.

When a detachment of British troops was seen to move upriver to a position near Fort Edward, Gates mistakenly believed that the whole of the British army would follow and hastily prepared to assault what he believed would be the rear guard of the departing troops.

The Americans moved from their position on the morning of October 9, covered by a dense fog that shrouded the valley. Daniel Morgan's brigade on

British six-pounder cannon at Saratoga, New York. *Photo by the author.*

the left flank had crossed the river on the upper reaches, and Learned with his men soon followed. Glover's and Nixon's Brigades were prepared to cross downriver when a handful of Glover's men encountered a British deserter, who told them that the troops were walking into a confrontation with nearly the entirety of the British army entrenched in the heights above them.

Glover quickly halted his brigade and sent one man back to warn General Gates and another to alert General Learned. Nixon's men had already begun crossing, and the brigadier general used his mirror to flash a message to the commander to pull back his men. Nixon halted his advance, but at the same time the fog dispersed and revealed the troops below the gleaming British cannons. The firing began before the men could re-cross the Fishkill to safety, and several of the soldiers were killed. Learned's men also had to scramble for safety under enemy fire, but the American assault was halted before what would surely have been a disastrous route of the troops.

General Gates moved quickly to enclose any avenue of escape, and by the sixteenth, the British had agreed to General Gates's conditions of surrender. The following day, Glover's Brigade was given the task of escorting General Burgoyne and the British prisoners of war to army headquarters in Cambridge, Massachusetts. But within days of these orders, Glover received word that his son, John, had been lost at sea. The effect of this loss was likely the reason the usually competent commander drifted from his responsibilities.

Rather than oversee the transport of the prisoners, Glover divided the body of prisoners into three groups, each of which would travel to Massachusetts under three separate routes, and left the task to his junior officers. He then

Illustration of Burgoyne's surrender, as printed in *American Heritage Magazine. Courtesy of the Smithsonian Institute.*

took a trip to Albany with Major General Friedrich Adolph von Riedesel, the ranking officer of the captured Hessian prisoners, where they dined at the mansion of General Schuyler and extended his stay for a week.

While Glover was on his vacation, the planned transport of prisoners became a fiasco. "Little or no effort was made to find sleeping quarters for the captives along the way. Prisoners were frequently forced to sleep in the open country in freezing weather....Exposed to the terrible cold of the mountains in western Massachusetts, two prisoners and some of the horses...froze to death one evening."[157]

By the time Glover rendezvoused with his brigade in Worcester, he had received a rare rebuke for his laxness in leadership. Glover took steps to improve the remainder of the march and spent much of that time with General Burgoyne, buoying the defeated general's spirits during the difficult trip of some 215 miles on horseback.

The brigade herded the prisoners into Boston under the peal of bells, surrounded by a large, cheering crowd. They reached the cantonment, where the prisoners were handed over to Colonel William R. Lee, a former officer under Glover in the Fourteenth Massachusetts.

Glover would linger in Cambridge, attempting to reconcile accounts from expenses during the march. As the troops had advanced from Saratoga to Cambridge, they had left a mountain of unpaid bills in their wake. In addition, scores of civilian complaints of damages needed to be addressed.

Nor was Glover anxious to return to a military encampment. He dallied in the comforts of the city and delayed answering Washington's request to join him at Valley Forge. Glover proffered his resignation, but the commander-in-chief would not consent. The low pay that officers received was beginning to take a toll, and the "spirit of resigning" commissions had, according to Washington, reached almost epidemic proportions.

Weeks passed in a tense silence between the two, with Glover having every intent on returning to Marblehead and Washington expecting his appearance at winter encampment. In the January 1778 session of Congress, Glover's name was put forward to lead an expedition into Canada. When he did finally recover and return to the army in June, he was given temporary command of West Point, and his brigade was formally handed over to Colonel Lee.

Within weeks, he was ordered to march to Rhode Island and assist with the transport of supplies for the coming Rhode Island campaign that summer. On August 1, Glover received a letter from General John Sullivan

View of Quaker Hill from Butts Hill, Portsmouth, Rhode Island. *From* Lossing's Pictorial History of the American Revolution.

with instructions to "please proceed to Boston, Marblehead and such other places as you may think proper to engage two or three hundred Seamen or other persons well acquainted with Boats, who are to act as Boatmen in the Expedition against Rhode Island."

Glover's newly formed brigade would join with the brigade under James Mitchell Varnum and the Continental troops under the Marquis de Lafayette. Washington would also send General Nathanael Greene back to his home state to bolster the command of General Sullivan.

In an effort to wrest back the island of Newport from British hands, plans had been laid for an all-out siege, with the assistance of the French navy as well as regiments of amphibious assault troops who would land on Conanicut Island (now Jamestown, Rhode Island) and use that as a staging ground to cut off the west passage from Newport and make a landing to attack Butts Hill, a British redoubt on the north end of the island. The Americans were to land on the eastern shore of Aquidneck Island and make their assault toward the British fortress along the roads that led from there.

Two roads on Aquidneck led straight to the British fort: the West Road, which began at the crossing from the Bristol Ferry, and the East Road, which was reached by the road from Howland's Ferry, where the fort lay just ahead of the bridge across the tidal pool at Easton's Point. The Americans would cross from Howland's Ferry and make their landing on the eastern shore, taking these two roads toward the British defenses to the north.

On August 9, the French commander Admiral Comte d'Estaing began disembarking troops on Conanicut Island. The British, who had ascertained the American plan, pulled back from Butt's Hill to their fortifications. General Sullivan, believing that he should take advantage of the situation, struck out at once to occupy the redoubt, much to the consternation of the French officers, who felt that Sullivan had left them vulnerable at such a distance. Upon hearing word that a British fleet was en route for reinforcement, D'Estaing recalled his troops and set out at once to meet the enemy fleet.

Sullivan was determined to press ahead with the attack, and on the tenth, he assigned the officers their duties. Glover was given command of the entire left division of the first line within the American camp.[158] The assault would begin with the firing of a cannon at dawn on August 12. The advance line would be composed of Glover's Brigade on the left flank, General Ezekial Cornell's brigade left of center and Colonel Christopher Greene's troops right of center, with General Varnum's brigade covering the right flank.

The troops had the entirety of the eleventh to prepare ammunition, their rations and supplies. At 4:00 p.m., the entire army paraded before Sullivan in a show of readiness. But as often happens in New England, a change in the weather stalled their plans.

Glover and the other troops awoke the morning of the twelfth to a fierce gale that bore heavy winds and rain that soaked the tents and clothing and, more important, ruined much ammunition and left the muskets useless. Such was the gale that it left the French fleet's sails and halyards in tatters, and D'Estaing pulled them back to Boston for repairs, with a promise to return.

The Americans were now paralyzed and at the mercy of the storm. When it abated after two days, word came from headquarters to prepare to march as before on August 15. That day also dawned bright and clear, and the march soon began with the first line advancing as planned, with Glover's Brigade advancing down the East Road, Varnum's Continentals taking the West Road and troops under Generals Greene and Cornell marching over stone walls and through the meadows between the two roads. By noon, they were within a mile and a half from the enemy lines. Here the troops halted and began the planned siege.

While waiting for the French fleet to return, the Americans were in a precarious position. Even as they marched, it appeared that General Sullivan was wavering on whether to continue the assault. Consulting his officers, Glover favored continuing the siege but also suggested taking steps to secure the forts at the northern end of the island close to the ferry in the event that an amphibious retreat became necessary. Glover's entire plan, revealed after the war, was to send a small force in boats to storm the British redoubt at the head of Easton's Beach and, once that was taken, to storm the beach itself and breach the defenses in front of Newport.

Sullivan considered the matter carefully but considered his army in its current state to be too weak to launch such an assault, and late on the fifteenth, Glover was called away from his brigade and given command of the Salem Volunteers and the Boston Independents, two militia units that contained experienced boatmen.

By the twentieth, however, their terms of service had expired, and the general issued a plea to those "spirited Citizens of Salem, Marblehead, etc. who so cheerfully turned out to take care of the boats."[159]

On the twenty-fourth, the Salem Volunteers were ordered to march to Howland's Ferry, where they were to "guard the boats and to man them when occasion may require." The men then came under command of William R. Lee, who had served as Glover's second in command during the battles at Long Island and Trenton.

The retreat began as darkness descended on the island on August 28. Glover's Brigade marched back up the East Road and rendezvoused with the other troops in the vicinity of Butt's Hill. Sullivan had his left extend to the East Road, the right to West Road and covering parties on each flank. Glover took headquarters in a house that lay just east of the foot of Quaker Hill.

Just after dawn on the morning of the twenty-ninth, the British noticed the retreat of the Americans and began their pursuit, and a heavy cannonade lobbed toward the new position taken by Sullivan's army. Glover and other officers were hastily eating breakfast and gulping down coffee when the cannonade began. Horses were already saddled at the door, and Glover sent his aide-de-camp, Rufus King, to reconnoiter the British pursuit. King stepped from the table, and his seat was taken by an officer named Sherburne. Moments later, a cannon ball flew into the room from an open window, missing the officers at the table but smashing into the unfortunate Sherburne's foot.

What the officers soon found was that at that very moment, the rear guard and pickets of the American army were putting up a fierce fight as General Smith sent up reinforcements and brought the American guns into position. Glover quickly rallied his brigade at their assigned position north of the crossroad between the end of West Road, and the East Road before the narrowing of the island to the peninsula known as Common Sense Point.

At the crest of Quaker Hill, Colonel Edward Wiggleworth's brigade had taken a heavy pounding but held the hill until an advance guard of Hessians attempted to cut off a path of retreat. Once alerted, the men flew downhill, past the abatis where Tyler's Brigade lay crouched and ready to fire, and streamed into the ranks of Glover's Brigade.

The Battle of Rhode Island, illustrated by Alan H. Archambault and featuring soldiers of the First Rhode Island Regiment. *Courtesy of the Rhode Island Society of the Sons of the American Revolution.*

At once the brigade's artillery, along with the First Rhode Island Regiment to Glover's right, sent a barrage of fire at the oncoming British and German troops. Sullivan would later praise both regiments for repulsing the attacks. With troops crouched behind stone walls and the artillery wreaking havoc on the field, by four o'clock in the afternoon the British and Hessian troops had withdrawn and regrouped around Quaker Hill, where the British artillery continued to fire on the American lines.

The following morning, the Americans quickly worked to evacuate the island. Glover would not be directly involved with this amphibious operation, but he had trained the Salem Volunteers and other boatmen well in the days before the retreat. As Billias wrote, "The amphibious retreat was beautifully executed; it was carried out in the face of the enemy, whose forces now outnumbered Sullivan's on land, and whose ships commanded local waters. The operation went off without a hitch and was completed by two in the morning without the loss of a single man, a piece of artillery, or of any important military stores."[160]

Rhode Island was Glover's last battlefield service. He resigned his commission again and returned to Marblehead, but he was, as before, persuaded by Washington to return, only to find the men under his command battle weary. He barely had the energy to lead them, and the ensuing mutiny, described in an earlier chapter, was a somber footnote to the career of an otherwise brilliant and brave commander in the field, as well as to the men he led who proved their bravery in whatever battle lay before them, be it be on land or water.

Chapter 7

JOHN STARK AND THE NEW HAMPSHIRE MILITIA

By the time of the Revolutionary War, John Stark was a seasoned veteran of the French and Indian War who had risen to the rank of brigadier general of the New Hampshire militia.

Stark owned and operated a sawmill and had raised a family of seven children in the town of Derryfield, New Hampshire. When news reached him of the shots fired at Lexington, he and his wife were expecting another child. Although plenty of reasons were readily apparent for him to remain at home, according to his biographer, word came to him while he was at the sawmill. He then went home, retrieved his musket and three dollars and set out to gather his men.

Traversing the southern half of the colony, by the time he reached the encampment at Winter Hill in Medford, one thousand men followed Stark. The volunteers of New Hampshire, like so many others, were ill equipped to undertake a prolonged campaign. They were short of uniforms, weapons and medical supplies.

Stark wrote at once to the Council of Safety in New Hampshire to apprise it of his situation. He was disappointed, then, when the requested weapons were delivered but no blankets, clothing or medical supplies. Writing again to the council, he learned in its reply that he had been replaced as overall commander by Nathaniel Fulsom, another New Hampshire man who had risen through the ranks of the militia.

The council assured Stark, however, that a commission, with command of a regiment, was available to him. As he had led the New Hampshire men this far, Stark swallowed his pride and took the post. By May 27, 1775, he and his men were undertaking their first assignment: to rescue the sheep and cattle on Hog and Noddle's Islands in Boston Harbor from British raids. Stark's men were joined by volunteers from Connecticut under command of General Israel Putnam.

As the islands were just spits of land rich with grasses, the settlers of Boston had long led their livestock at low tide to the islands for grazing.

The objective that morning, undertaken by six hundred troops and two four-pound cannons hauled through the surf by horses, was to drive as many of the livestock as they could back to the mainland before being noticed. They were stunningly successful.

By 2:30 p.m., they had herded most of the sheep to Chelsea. Stark and his men had maneuvered their way to Noddle's Island and had driven off a fair number of cattle and horses before they came under fire. At the same time, a British schooner, a sloop and twelve barks with guns maneuvered into the channel to cut off an American retreat.

Stark got his men back to shore and found cover from which they could fire back at the British vessels and prevent an assault onshore. In the fray, the British schooner *Dina* became bottled up in the shallow waters and was soon

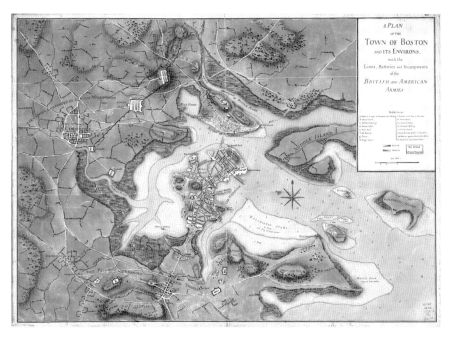

A Plan of the Town of Boston. From Carrington's Battles of the American Revolution.

a sitting duck for the Americans. They fired at the crew desperately trying to tow the schooner to deeper water. The Connecticut men under Putnam waded into the water and forced the crew to abandon their efforts and the ship. The men ransacked the vessel and set it ablaze.

The role his men had played in the "Battle of Chelsea," as it became known, landed him new respect in the council when he appeared before it and the New Hampshire Congress in June to plead his case to be given back his senior command. It was a winning argument. He returned to Cambridge as colonel of the "1st Regiment of New Hampshire for the Defense of America."[161]

On June 17, the battle for Boston began in earnest with both artillery and cannon fire, which began at five o'clock in the morning. The Americans had placed their forces in a semicircle around Boston. They choked off any route to the country from Boston Neck and erected an impressive collection of artillery on Dorchester Heights to the south, Bunker Hill and to the north, across the Charles River on the highest point of land on Charlestown Neck.[162]

Stark's regiment heard the cannonade from its encampment and waited for orders to reinforce the troops at Boston. He received word late in the morning to send "a detachment of 200 men, with proper officers to their assistance." Stark sent the detachment under the command of Colonel Wyman, and after their departure, he rode out to the Neck accompanied by Major McClary. What they witnessed convinced them that the remainder of the regiment would soon be needed as well. But as they returned, they encountered some of the men just sent out "resting in the fields." The commander angrily rebuked their lackluster response and rode back with speed to Mendon to prepare his troops.

He found the men were "destitute of ammunition," and so a gill cup of powder with fifteen balls and one fuse were given to each man. Those who had cartridge boxes spent the afternoon making cartridges. The rest stored the powder in powder horns and the balls in a small sack hung from a belt.

The remainder of Stark's men set out for the battlefield at one o'clock, with Commander Stark and Colonel Dearborn both on foot. The New Hampshire column made its way deliberately to Charlestown Neck through the cannonade and fire.

Massachusetts soldier Samuel Blachley Webb wrote to his brother and described the scene on Breed's Hill in vivid detail: "Thro the cannonading of the Ships, Bombs, Chain Shot, Ring Shot, & Double headed Shot flew thick as Hail Stones,—but thank Heaven, few of our men suffered, by them, but when we mounted the summit where the Engagement was,—Good God how the balls flew."[163]

Pushing through a mob of reluctant soldiers, Major McClary cleared a path for the New Hampshire regiment to pass through. Stark led the men across the Neck under heavy fire. When they reached the position held by General Putnam but received no orders, Stark took the initiative and led his men downhill to fill a gap on the American line. He ordered Captain John Moore to take his company to the bank of the Mystic River, where they quickly constructed a dry rock wall behind which his marksmen could take cover. The remainder of the regiment lay behind a rail fence, firing downhill at the enemy slowly advancing through the newly mown meadows.

Lines of British regulars advanced up the hill toward Dearborn and Stark's men. Along the Mystic River Beach, a landing party of Royal Welsh Fusiliers was followed by the King's Own Fourth Regiment of Foot.

Behind the hastily constructed stone wall, Moore's marksmen waited for the enemy's approach. Colonel Stark had walked out and marked a distinctive spot with a stake in the ground, ordering that the men should not fire until the marching fusiliers reached that point.

The men displayed remarkable discipline as the enemy approached closer, and when they reached the stake Spark had set in the ground, they rose as one to deliver a blistering attack that "gave such a deadly fire as cut down every man of the party opposed to them."[164] The British regulars struggled in vain to regroup as the marksmen made targets of those officers attempting to rally the troops with shouts, gestures and waving of their swords.

A third attack from the regulars came by way of a bayonet charge aimed at Prescott's position. This time the British succeeded in breaching the breastworks and the American line and took many of the men attempting to flee prisoner.

The Americans had run out of ammunition, and Preston, Knowlton and Stark hastily organized the withdrawal. It was ultimately decided that the New Hampshire men would stay and cover the retreat of the Massachusetts and Connecticut soldiers. After moving his men out of firing range, Stark wondered aloud if the British were in pursuit. Major McClary volunteered to return and assess the situation.

When McClary returned to the Neck, he saw the British already digging trenches on the hill previously occupied by the Americans. But before he could return and tell the news to Stark, a cannonball fired from a British ship in the harbor struck him dead.

In his report issued two days after the Battle of Bunker Hill, Stark told the New Hampshire Congress that he had lost fifteen men dead or missing in the fray, with another forty-five wounded. Still, he declared himself satisfied that the enemy, in his estimation, suffered three times the losses of Americans.

The New Hampshire Congress also received letters from Nathaniel Fulsom, the man Congress had placed in charge of New Hampshire forces. Fulsom wrote his own secondhand account of the battle, as he was never in the field, and complained of Stark's insubordination in refusing to hand in a return of his men in a timely fashion.

Fulsome wrote that Stark "does not intend to be under subordination to any person appointed by the Congress of New Hampshire." The Congress duly ignored Fulsom's fuming letter. It undoubtedly knew of Stark's contempt for the political appointments seemingly doled out by the dozens as the army expanded that spring of 1775.

By midseason, illness in the form of camp fever had begun plaguing the encampments. Stark and the men from New Hampshire remained on garrison duty and engaged in occasional skirmishes as the British sent troops on forays to find supplies, although both sides suffered by summer from illness and hunger as the siege continued.

Pressure grew on Washington and his officers to take action outside Boston and shake the lethargy that had crept into the war. Plans for an expedition into Canada were quickly made, pushed by General Benedict Arnold, who was sure that he could strike a blow to the British to the north.

While Stark's men may have resented having to stay behind at the encampment, they were surely relieved when word reached them of the disastrous march through the wilderness and the American defeat months later.

By year's end in Boston, the men of the First New Hampshire regiment were finishing their term of service to the army, yet they had not been paid for several months. The men's suspicions soon fell on the paymaster, one Colonel Samuel Hobart. When a mob of soldiers grabbed Hobart at his headquarters and brought him before Stark to air their complaints, the commander calmly heard them out and refused to punish them for their actions.

Not surprisingly, Hobart did take action and fired off a complaint to his political superiors, who passed it along to Washington. A court of inquiry was subsequently held, but rather than relieve Stark of his command, the court accepted a written apology.

As the year turned, the Americans were buoyed by the arrival of fresh recruits and especially by Colonel Henry Knox's troops from Fort Ticonderoga, who had achieved the remarkable feat of hauling forty-three cannons and fourteen smaller guns across the frozen Hudson River on sleds and then over the Berkshire Mountains to Framingham, outside Boston. These were moved into place along strategic points around the besieged town. Americans occupied Dorchester Heights once again in early March, and as the ground was too frozen to dig trenches, they struck up man-made blinds to hide the guns that now gave them an easy target of the British position. The Americans put the guns into place so clandestinely that it went unnoticed until the sixteenth of the month.

Around three o'clock in the morning on the following day, the British began forming columns in the streets of Boston and marching to the waterfront. By nine o'clock in the morning, the ships that had long held Boston Harbor were leaving, and the occupying troops departed with them.

Stark heard of the departure and toured the ruins of the redoubt where Prescott's men had held their ground for so long. He, along with Colonel Rees and Captain James Wilkinson, walked through the blackened ruins of Charlestown and then rowed across the river, where they found a narrow, winding lane leading into Boston.[165]

Just a few days later, having received orders to lead two Continental regiments into Norwich, Connecticut, and await further instructions there, Stark left with an advance party of troops on March 20. In April, Washington chose New Hampshire general John Sullivan to lead an expedition north, with troops that included Stark's New Hampshire regiment. While the troops had been sent ahead, the officers dallied. Stark paid a visit to his wife and newborn child in Derryfield and Sullivan lingered in the state until the twenty-seventh, and in fact, the two officers may have traveled together to St. John's in Quebec.

On May 30, a council of war was convened at Fort Chambly, which the Americans had captured the previous September. The officers concurred that the army should continue the campaign in Canada. Sullivan officially took over command of the army on June 1 and wrote a cautionary letter to John Hancock and Congress concerning the condition of his army: "I am extremely sorry to inform you, that from the officers whose business it was to give Congress the true state of matters, Congress has not, I believe, received anything like it."

Everything was in confusion, and the troops were frightened of the coming campaign, as the army in the north had "dwindled into a mob without even

Fort Chambly, Quebec Province. *Courtesy of Norman Desmarais.*

the form or order of regularity." Despite these conditions, Sullivan went ahead with plans to attack Trois Rivières across the St. Lawrence River. Stark vehemently opposed the plan, believing it to be hazardous and imprudent considering the condition of the army. Sullivan pressed ahead, and Stark obeyed orders despite his misgivings, which proved to be correct. The general placed 600 troops under command of Colonel Arthur St. Clair and another 1,600 to follow under the command of General William Thompson.

The attack proved to be disastrous from the start, when the American troops crossing the St. Lawrence were spotted by Quebec militia, which sent the alarm to the British forces. Thompson left 450 men at the riverbank and took the remainder to confront what he believed to be a small force of British regulars.

Once across, the Americans were led by a local farmer through swampland, allowing the British to position themselves behind the American lines. They also dispatched the HMS *Martin* and other ships to Pointe du Lac, which drove the Americans from their positions. A column of men under General Anthony Wayne managed to make it out of the swamp and confront a force of regulars under British general Simon Fraser, but the Americans were outnumbered. After a brief exchange, Wayne's men fled the scene, leaving their guns and ammunition behind. As they fled into the woods, they soon became bottlenecked between the British troops, whose firing kept them from the escape route, and the ships at Pointe du Lac, which continued a barrage of firing into the woods where his men lay hidden.[166]

When St. Clair retreated to the river crossing, he found it occupied by the British. They retreated to the woods, and only by fleeing upriver did they avoid capture. General Thompson was not so fortunate. He and seventeen of his officers were taken prisoner, and British troops rounded up more of his men straggling through the woods in the days that followed.

General Wayne managed to rally a rear guard of about 800 men, which confronted the British and allowed a staggered retreat, but in all, 236 Americans were taken prisoner, with 30 to 50 men killed during the exchanges.

On the night of June 13, another council was held at Sullivan's headquarters, where it was decided to withdraw from the province and make a stand at Fort Ticonderoga. The retreat began the next day, with those soldiers in good health rowing the Sorel River toward Lake Champlain, while others marched along the riverbank. Those on the river struggled to ferry the combined weight of the men, arms and baggage down the length of the St. Lawrence. Where the river became shallow, the men had to climb out and drag the boats against the shallow current and those gravel banks exposed above the water.

John Stark wrote that "in our retreat from Sorrel, I brought up the rear to Crown Point, was left with a great deal of the stores and about 30 men only to assist me, and the Regulars very often within five miles of us."

In the retreat, the men torched sawmills, whatever boats encountered and Fort Chambly itself before continuing on to St. John's, where Sullivan's forces met those of Benedict Arnold, who had attempted to burn Montreal and Fort St. Jean before departing. All agreed that they should leave Canada with the greatest haste and, in Arnold's words, "secure our own country before it is too late."

Not all agreed with Arnold. One officer, surgeon Dr. Lewis Beebe, was charged with tending those in the regiment infected with smallpox. He wrote often and openly of his feelings about the treatment of the troops and the decisions and general behavior of the officers of the northern army, writing on June 10, "No intelligence of importance comes to hand this day; except orders, from the great Mr. Brigadier General Arnold, for Colonel Poor with his regiment to proceed to Sorrell immediately: Is this not a politick plan,

Left: Illustration of General John Stark. *From* Lossing's Pictorial History of the Revolutionary War.

Below: Postcard of Lake Champlain as seen from Mount Defiance. *From the author's collection.*

especially since there is not Ten men in the regiment, but what has either now got the smallpox; or taken the infection. Some men love to command, however ridiculous their orders may appear."[167]

The many sick soldiers among the Americans were ferried to Isle aux Noix (Nut Island) in the Sorrel River just above the entrance to Lake Champlain, where conditions continued to worsen. Many had fallen ill with smallpox, and as the days progressed, many grew worse and died. A large pit was dug on the island into which fresh bodies of dead soldiers were rolled each day and covered, awaiting the next group of fatalities.

Stark was among the handful of healthy troops on the island, being immune from previous exposure to the disease. On June 20, he organized the evacuation of the ill to Crown Point and was among the last to leave the infected island.[168]

The month of July brought days of heat, humidity and fierce thunderstorms that brought only temporary relief. Dr. Lewis Beebe, who treated the soldiers stricken with smallpox, wrote, "This is a remarkable Cuntry for thunder and lightening [*sic*]…this is the 9th day since my arrival here, during which time we have had it severely every day."[169]

The son of Connecticut governor John Trumbull would find "not an army but a mob, the shattered remains of twelve or fifteen fine battalions ruined by sickness, fatigue and desertion." At the same time, Congress moved to replace the command of General Sullivan in favor of General Horatio Gates. Washington, and some in Congress concurred with him, believed that as a commander, Sullivan held "an over desire of being popular" with his men, a position that many believed would invariably lead to a lack of discipline among the troops.

Sullivan was a popular leader, and news of his replacement plunged morale among the troops and junior officers. Dr. Beebe believed that the move "most likely will finally cause them [the officers] to finally resign their commissions; then we Shall be in a fine pickle to meet the enemy."[170]

On July 6, the generals of the northern army met to discuss the merits of moving the army to Fort Ticonderoga and a wooded hillock across the narrows below the southern end of Lake Champlain on the Vermont border.

Based on surveillance by the twenty-year-old Deputy Adjunct General John Trumbull, but without consulting their field officers, the generals decided that "all the healthy and uninfected troops…retire immediately to the strong ground on the East side of the Lake, opposite to Ticonderoga." Those still ravaged by illness would be moved to Fort George, on the southern end of the lake.

The decision took the field officers by surprise, and John Stark was among the first to react. His signature would be the first of twenty-two colonels who wrote and signed a "Remonstrance" delivered to General Schuyler. The field officers cited seven reasons that they believed made a strong case for staying in place at Crown Point. A few of them addressed reasons that had seemingly been ignored by the higher command: while the fort they currently occupied was in ruins, so too was Ticonderoga, and there, in the midst of a "howling wilderness," they would lose the naval superiority they held in the northern reaches of the lake. Another reason was that if they abandoned Crown Point, it would be nearly impossible to recapture, and the abandonment of the fort, as John Stark knew well, would leave the American settlements vulnerable to British attack, as they could easily use the road that led to and from the fort that Stark and his men had constructed during the French and Indian War.

The decision surprised Washington as well, who agreed with the contentious officers and wrote briskly to General Schuyler, "The reasons assigned against it by the field officers in their remonstrance coincide greatly with my own ideas and those of the other general officers I have had the opportunity of consulting with, and seem to be of considerable weight—I may add, conclusive."[171]

Washington's chief reason was his belief that once abandoned, Crown Point would quickly be taken by the enemy, and any naval advantage on Lake Champlain would be lost. More than this, he was disappointed that the argument failed to persuade the superior officers. Nonetheless, he let the commanders' decision stand, as to overrule it might "establish a precedent for the inferior officers to set up their judgment whenever they would in opposition to those of their superiors."

THE WITHDRAWAL WAS SOON underway, with the first concern being to ferry the sick to safety. Adjunct John Trumbull made the grim assessment that some 2,800 men, more than half of the force at the fort, were too ill to march. Counting the invalids within the constructed shelters of tents, sheds and "miserable brush huts," he recorded, "I can truly say that I did not look into a tent or hut in which I did not find a dead or dying man."[172]

Beginning on July 10, boatmen ferried the New England troops to the wooded hillside scouted by Trumbull, soon dubbed "Mount Independence," while the units from Pennsylvania encamped on the stubby peninsula below the fort.

Present-day scene of battle near Ticonderoga. *Courtesy of Norman Desmarais.*

The New Hampshire men were positioned at the new encampment on the hill, where they cleared the forest and constructed a stockade near a spring on the wide expanse of the hilltop, as well as huts and a hospital, with roads connecting these as well as the gun emplacements. They were soon joined by units from Connecticut and Massachusetts.

News of the signing of the Declaration of Independence buoyed the men's spirits, and the entire document was read aloud to cheers after services on July 28.

The men of both encampments spent the remainder of the summer preparing for the anticipated attack from the British. Part of that preparation was shipbuilding. General Schuyler had ordered that a site at Skenesborough, on the southern edge of the lake, be used to construct an American fleet for the northern army as the troops began their withdrawal from Canada. General Benedict Arnold and Colonel Jeduthan Baldwin were placed in charge of the operation.

Stark's biographers explained the tedious and dangerous process: "Shipwrights laid down the keels and lapped the planks on the craft at Skenesborough. Then crews rowed the hulls to Ticonderoga where the boats became naval vessels. Workers stepped the masts from each craft from atop a cliff beside the lake on Mount Independence. Then, sailors swarmed aloft to fix the standing and running rigging. [Standing rigging supports the masts, while running rigging raises and lowers the sails.] Finally, each boat was armed and equipped for war."[173]

In the meantime, redoubts were constructed for the artillery at Fort Ticonderoga and Mount Independence. But these lay in the shadow of another mountain overlooking the lesser hills and the outlet of Lake George. Trumbull in his surveillance report had recommended occupying and fortifying this hill as well. Called Mount Defiance, the generals believed the mountain impenetrable to British forces and dismissed the young adjunct's recommendations, even to the point of ridicule.

Such an oversight would become apparent in the coming year, but at present, Arnold had his navy in order and was given orders by Gates for a tentative surveillance of Lake Champlain. Arnold, however, relished the idea of a confrontation with the British fleet. He wrote to General Gates that his ships anchored the length of a mile along the narrow western channel off Valcour Island, were "as near together as possible, & in such form that few Vessels can attack us at the same Time & then will be exposed to the fire of the whole fleet."

Arnold got what he wished for, but the outcome was less than what he had anticipated. When British ships cruised past the southern end of the island in early October, they took no notice of the fleet. But upon turning back, they noticed the fleet anchored between the island and New York.

ON OCTOBER 11, THE flotillas faced off in a battle that lasted eight hours. Arnold later calculated that he had lost sixty men before the remaining American fleet, under cover of darkness, secured its sails and used muffled oars to make its escape, retreating in the direction of the abandoned Crown Point. The British vessels pursued and captured several more ships before Arnold, aboard the *Congress*, led the surviving ships into what is now called Arnold Bay in Vermont territory, where he ordered the sailors to abandon and scuttle their ships.

The sailors made their way back along the bank until rescue boats came for them. Fortunately for them, the British did not pursue the men on shore but instead kept a distance and fired half-heartedly at the shoreline. As the Americans continued to anticipate an attack on Ticonderoga, the men there were engaged in fashioning a boom that stretched across the narrows between the fort and Mount Independence. There were even further plans to build a bridge above the boom, so that reinforcements could cross from one artillery encampment to the other.

The days seemed to pass in false alarms and rumors of when the British planned to attack or move back into Canada. The Americans had hunkered down in huts with stoves to stay warm. The British encampment still lay in canvas tents, although their activity of rowing on the lake and taking soundings seemed to augment an impending attack.

That day seemed to come on the morning of October 28 when twenty-eight sails appeared on the lake a short distance away. Dr. Lewis Beebe recorded, "This morning at 8 o'clock the alarm was given soon after which several sail, and a number of boats hove in sight, all which landed at 3 mile point. One of their boats received a few merry shot from our Batteries for Coming too near us."[174]

Beebe recorded the following day that the British had removed from the point the evening before, although the troops expected them to return, perhaps in greater number. There was confidence, however, that they would be prepared. Beebe wrote that same day that "[t]he militia come in by the hundreds."

Sergeant Roger Lamb of the British forces under General Guy Carleton wrote in his memoir that "the strength of that garrison and the season of the year restrained us from making any attempt, at that time on Ticonderoga."

Within a few days, scouts would discover that the British had left Crown Point and were headed north into Canada.

Once the Canadian campaign ended, thousands of troops began a staggered withdrawal from Fort Ticonderoga and Mount Independence. Although the troops were sorely needed in New York, in order to prevent the roads from being clogged with soldiers, horses and wagons, the withdrawal was a lengthy process. The New Hampshire men left on November 14, with those fit soldiers of the regiment marching to Fort George and the remainder, still classified as invalid, sent home.

John Stark also returned home to Derryfield to take care of his long-neglected family. His two eldest sons, Caleb and Alexander, were still serving with units in the war, but there were still six other minor children at home. His wife, Molly, was pregnant with their ninth child and had only their thirteen-year-old son to help with chores.

Stark also returned home to give the wages due Matthew Patten to his family, as the soldier had died before receiving them. In one of the cruel twists of fate the war would bring to families, at the height of the smallpox epidemic at Ticonderoga and Mount Independence, a small fortune in overdue wages arrived for many of those who lay sick and dying.

In late November, Stark would rejoin the remnants of his regiment as they marched with other New England troops who had served at Ticonderoga, south through the forests and mountains near the Delaware River in New York.[175]

The men soon found themselves in dire conditions. Many of the men had a scarcity of clothing, including shoes and blankets. Weather continued to worsen, and the encampment found itself isolated from any news of the war. Major James Wilkinson, aide to General Gates, recalled, "The winter had set in with severity: our troops were bare of clothing; numbers barefoot and without tents, provisions or transport of any kind. The men and officers sought shelter wherever they could find it in that thinly settled tract. We were halted on the 11th [of December] by a heavy fall of snow, which increased the General's anxiety for information from General Washington, and so to relieve his solicitude, I volunteered my services to find him."[176]

Stark's men were engaged along with others in collecting boats along a seventy-mile stretch of the river, to either use in ferrying troops or supplies or to burn and keep from British hands. These regiments would regroup along the west bank of the Delaware while Washington waited for reinforcements from Generals Lee and Gates.

Word of Lee's capture soon came to the commander-in-chief, and he still had no word as to Gates's location. Men's enlistments expired daily, and hordes of soldiers would depart at year's end. Congress, fearful of an attack on Philadelphia, had fled to Baltimore. All this precipitated the need for action be taken within the next two weeks if the army were to strike a blow before winter closed its icy grip on the northern states.

The New Hampshire regiment arrived at the American encampment on December 20. On Christmas Eve, Stark and the other officers—Colonels Henry Knox and John Glover and Generals Nathanael Greene, John Sullivan and Horatio Gates—met to discuss the finalized plans for the attack on Hessian-held Trenton, New Jersey.

Stark learned that his men would be the spearhead of the right flank under General Sullivan, while General Greene would lead the left flank into battle.

Late on Christmas Day, the New Hampshire men gathered with others, warmed themselves by a makeshift fire and listened to an officer read a stirring passage from Thomas Paine, urging them "not to shrink from the service" of their country, before marching to their designated crossing point.

When the army had completed its crossing, the men gathered again and began the march to Trenton. After roughly five miles, the men separated into two divisions, with Washington and Greene leading troops diverting along a path to the Pendleton Road and the upper part of the town, while Sullivan, with Stark's and Glover's Brigade, continued along the River Road.

It was a difficult march, as a blizzard had descended at the moment of their crossing the river, and those roads not covered with a glaze of ice were torn up into muck and snow—making the hauling of the artillery pieces especially slow. As the men marched, word was passed down to fix bayonets, as the muskets were too wet to fire and much of the ammunition had become damp and useless.

A company of local farmers and New Jersey militiamen led Stark and his soldiers into town. As they reached the outskirts of Trenton, they encountered a picket of Hessians. As they came within firing range of the pickets, they heard the shouts and shots from Greene's men entering the town a few blocks away. If this did not unnerve the Hessians, the planned bayonet charge by the regiments caused them to flee in panic to the streets. James Wilkinson later wrote, "The enemy made a momentary shew of resistance by a wild and undirected fire from the windows of their quarters which they abandoned as we advanced."

The artillery rowed across the river and hauled into place by the units quickly proved its worth, wreaking carnage on the Hessians and disrupting any attempt to rally a defense of the town. When the smoke from the cannons had cleared, the American forces had captured 886 men, as well was 23 officers. The report sent to Congress a few days after the battle estimated that "not more than thirty" of the enemy had been killed, as they had never had the chance to organize an armed resistance.

Washington was content to take these blessings of good fortune and resisted any talk from his officers of pursuing the British. The soldiers were ordered to return to camp by nightfall. It was a wise decision. The men were extremely fatigued and, moreover, had confiscated forty hogshead of rum in town, and many became so inebriated they would have been useless in battle and likely killed. The loss of men was the last thing the army needed.

As Washington plotted in camp in Pennsylvania, some 1,800 men of the Pennsylvania Association arrived under General John Cadwalader. Their arrival buoyed the men and their commander, and Washington quickly convened another council of war at the home of Widow Harris, where they formulated a plan proposed by Cadwalader to return to Trenton and drive the British from West Jersey, "the success of which will raise an army next spring."[177]

This crossing was less dramatic though more difficult. Ice had thickened as the winter set in—men could literally walk across some of the embarkation points along the river—but horses and artillery still needed to be ferried by boat. Despite the difficulties, combined forces had come into Trenton by December 30. A hard freeze kept the fires burning brightly in camp the next few days.

The army anticipated an attack on the city by Cornwallis and had massed artillery behind the swollen Assunpink Creek and aimed cannons at the few crossing points. The arrival of regular and Hessian troops on the outskirts of the town on January 2 set off skirmishes along the roads to Trenton and Princeton. The Americans held their ground until nightfall.

In another council held with their backs to the river, the officers decided on a bold strategy of attacking the town of Princeton rather than retreat once more across the Delaware. Early on the morning of January 3, 1777, Washington ordered a corps of four hundred men to remain in Trenton

Detail of painting by Edwin Austin Abbey of troops training in musket handling, as reproduced in *The Revolutionary War, America's Fight for Freedom*, published by the National Geographic Society, 1967. *Photo by the author.*

stoking the fires, so that the British would believe the entire army still remained in place.

Washington took four hundred men and officers onto the now frozen road to Princeton. The Americans "marched with great silence and order," Henry Knox wrote, and the solid roads aided movement of his artillery as well. Reaching Stony Brook in the early morning, the order quickly evolved into battle conditions as a forward detachment under Brigadier General Mercer encountered the first British regulars outside an apple orchard, where a fierce fight soon erupted.

The Americans fell back but were rallied by Washington's appearance on the scene, riding into the thick of the firefight and rallying the troops to regroup and pursue the retreating redcoats.

The New Hampshire men were likely with Sullivan's troops who marched into the center of town while fighting erupted in the southwest. When British soldiers took refuge in Nassau Hall on the college campus and fired at the Americans from the windows. Captain Alexander Hamilton calmly placed a battery aimed at the front of the hall and opened fire, while troops under Captain James Moore stormed the main door. Those inside quickly surrendered.

As they faced the close of another year, the matter of the expiration of service once again came to the forefront. Officers were urged to rally their men for reenlistment—what would such a recent victory mean if half the army suddenly went home? Washington convinced Treasurer Robert Morris in Pennsylvania to somehow find and send cash to be used for bonuses sent to Trenton.

Stark's men needed more persuasion. When he addressed his men, he called up the memory of their actions in the battles for Boston and Mount Independence and promised to sell his own farm to pay their overdue wages if Congress failed to send them. He proposed they enlist for another six weeks, and so persuasive was his argument, and so respected was he, that every single soldier of the regiment signed on to serve.

Following the winter campaign of 1776, John Stark returned to New Hampshire to recruit for his regiment. Once there, he learned that he had been passed over once again for promotion, and in response to this, he resigned his commission and stayed home. General Sullivan attempted to persuade him to return to the field but only received a promise that Stark would return if there was the threat of a British invasion from Canada.

By mid-June 1777, the Americans had learned that such a threat was very real. British general John Burgoyne, along with some ten thousand troops, was making his way down Lake Champlain toward Ticonderoga.

An invading force of some eight thousand men had set out from Quebec on June 17 in hundreds of bateaux. The British plan was to seize Crown Point, then Ticonderoga and then Fort Edward before an assault on Albany. If successful, the plan would divide the eastern colonies from the southern and, more importantly, cut off the supply routes for the American army.

But as with the best-laid plans, the New England weather sent them awry. The days became brutally hot, with relief only coming from tremendous thunderstorms that forced the troops to land and seek shelter. When the storms abated, mosquitoes and black flies tortured men. It took Burgoyne's flotilla nearly one month to reach the vicinity of Ticonderoga. When it did, a German surgeon noted in his journal, "The enemy has hoisted a red flag on the fort to express that they would rather lose their lives than their freedom."[178]

Use of a red swallowtail banner was internationally understood on land as a warning of military exercise and on sea to let other ships know that the vessel held munitions. Burgoyne expected a long siege and set his artillery in place while infantry units occupied land approaching Mount Defiance.

The Americans comprised a force of a mere 2,300 troops under General Arthur St. Clair, who petitioned each day for reinforcements of militia. The commander of the northern army, Horatio Gates, left St. Clair to his own devices and stayed firmly ensconced at Albany.

John Stark remained at Derryfield. He was kept apprised of the situation there by letters from his son Caleb Stark, who was there and fought in the ensuing battle, along with quartermaster Patrick Cogan.

St. Clair had prepared his defenses, erecting a boom across but neglecting once again to occupy Mount Defiance. Perhaps, as earlier officers had, the general had determined that the mountain was impenetrable, although this had been proven wrong on a reconnaissance expedition during the previous defense of the fort.

Burgoyne took advantage of the oversight and soon had sent a work party to hack and saw its way through vegetation and construct a pathway up the southwest side of the mountain. They then hauled up two twelve-pound cannons up the steep slope, utilizing nearly all the cattle they had confiscated to drag the guns into place.

On July 5, when St. Clair realized that the Americans were now vulnerable, he ordered the evacuations of the fort and Mount Independence before the British artillery had fired a shot. Dr. James Thatcher, the surgeon of the fort, recorded that the Americans left in such haste that "[a]ll our cannon, provisions and the bulk of our baggage…fell into the enemy's hands." In fact, a few cannons had left with the flotilla of boats carrying the sick and wounded, but the majority were left behind as St. Clair fled, leading his troops into the mountains of Vermont.

One Vermont commander, Colonel Seth Warner, and his Continental regiment of Green Mountain Boys brought up the rear of the retreat, along with Colonel Nathan Hale and the Second New Hampshire Regiment. With Burgoyne and his officers just a few miles away, Colonel Warner and the three regiments under his command encamped in the foothills of Hubbardton and prepared to slow the enemy's pursuit.

On the morning of July 7, the American sentries spied redcoats under General Simon Fraser ascending the hillside. They quickly assembled and formed defensive positions, exchanging fierce fire with Fraser's forces until reinforcements came to the British general's aid in the form of Brunswick auxiliaries, driving the Americans from their position into a wheat field and up Pittsfield Ridge, where they scattered into the forest.

Word of the American retreat came with the stragglers and deserters of St. Clair's army reaching Manchester, New Hampshire. The shock and shame of such a loss reverberated through the colonies, with most blaming St. Clair for a dismal show of defense. "There are some indeed," wrote surgeon James Thatcher, "who even accuse him of treachery." John Adams fired off a missive that declared, in part, "We shall never be able to defend a post until we shoot a general!"

In the aftermath of the battle, the delegates of the Vermont Republic assembled in Windsor and struggled to obtain weapons and ammunition. A Council of Safety was quickly formed to act as the interim government and gave it power to take military action. Within days, the council had written to its counterparts in New Hampshire that "the defenseless inhabitants [of Vermont] are heartily disposed to Defend their Liberties." But it was clear that they could not defend the state alone.

New Hampshire's assembly empathized with its neighbors but lacked the funds to raise any more troops than were already in the state militia. So fervent was the desire to come to Vermont's defense that the Speaker of the House rose to give a rousing speech in which he pledged more than enough money to fund a regiment and suggested to the assembly, "Our friend John Stark, who so nobly maintained the honor of our state at Bunker Hill, may be safely entrusted with the honor of the enterprise and we will check the progress of Burgoyne."

In giving Stark the command, the state explicitly ordered the commander to "march into the State of Vermont and there act in conjunction with the Troops of that State or any other of the States or of the United States or separately as it shall appear Expedient to you for the protection of the People or the annoyance of the enemy."

Stark accepted the command offered and rode to Exeter, New Hampshire, to take charge of recruitment. Word was sent to militia units throughout the neighboring counties, and 1,492 men and officers were raised for the defense of the state when a request came for reinforcements for the Continental regiment under Major General Benjamin Lincoln, the latest man who had been promoted over him.

Stark refused his request. Not on personal grounds, as some have suggested, but rather based on the militia's creed that its duty was the defense of its home state, and its detachment could only come if approved by the provincial government. Accordingly, the commander's refusal explained that he answered only to the New Hampshire Assembly, not the Continental Congress.

In the wake of the poor performance of Continental troops at Ticonderoga, Stark and the New Hampshire Assembly were wary of leaving the state vulnerable to attack. The commander clearly felt that, should Burgoyne decide to do so, he could raid the settlements in the Connecticut River Valley with impunity while the army waited out the enemy at Hudson Heights.

Josiah Bartlett, a member of the assembly who had appointed Stark, came briskly to his defense and reiterated those long-held beliefs: "Surely every State has a right to raise their militia for their own Defence against a Common Enemy and to put them under such Command as they shall think proper."

As events transpired, Stark was proven correct in his assumption that the resources in the Connecticut River Valley would be the target of the British quartermasters.

DURING THE FIRST WEEK of August, a detachment of some seven hundred troops under Lieutenant Frederick Baum and composed of Hessians, a small number of Brunswick dragoons, Canadians, Loyalists and Native Americans began to work its way into the disputed New Hampshire Grants territory to raid the area for horses, draft animals, provisions and other supplies.

By the thirteenth, they had raided farms from the Hudson to Cambridge, New York. Most of the farmers had driven off their horses, leaving their cattle and chickens for the raiders to take. The communities throughout the valley were on edge. The Hessians in other raids had been accused of pillaging and raping, and the Indians who came along with the raiders soon had a reputation for destroying everything in their path. As a result, the roads in the valley were soon thick with refugees.

Stark sent a detachment of two hundred men under Colonel William Gregg that soon met the raiders at Sancoick Mill. A firefight ensued, and when Gregg pulled his men back, a carpenter among them stayed behind and sabotaged the bridge leading over Little White Creek to slow the progress of Baum's troops.

When Stark received word that a large contingent of troops was marching toward Bennington, he moved his troops to a hill west of the town, overlooking the Walloomsac River, in full view of Baum's detachment.

When the German commander noticed Stark's position, he withdrew to a steep hill north of the river and set about building a redoubt of timber and stones. Hoping to lure the enemy troops onto the plain near the river, Stark had his men harass those the men guarding the bridge, as well as patrols that engaged in skirmishes around the British encampment, to demoralize the troops before the impending battle. One of these raids killed a Mohawk chief, who was buried with some ceremony at the British encampment.

In the meantime, Stark had moved his forces back to Bennington. Baum also inexplicably moved his men; rather than constructing a formidable redoubt and a strong defensive position, he split his troops into three units along the hillside, but so distant from one another that communications and coordination in the heat of the battle would prove impossible. Such was Baum's inexperience that common soldiers and even the surgeon accompanying the men came to question his judgment.

A prolonged rain dampened plans for an assault. Local militia units continued to arrive at camp, including the Berkshire County militia from Pittsfield, Massachusetts, and a detachment of the Green Mountain Boys from Manchester. The Americans now outnumbered Baum's detachment two to one.

On the morning of the sixteenth, a council of war was conducted with Stark and his field commanders. These included Seth Warner of the Green Mountain Boys; Colonel Samuel Herrick of the Vermont Rangers; Lieutenant Colonel Moses Nichols of Plymouth, New Hampshire; and two

Illustrated map of Bennington Heights. *From* Lossing's Pictorial History of the Revolutionary War.

other New Hampshire officers in Colonel David Hobart of Plymouth and Colonel Thomas Stickney of Concord.

Stark had decided to use an enveloping tactic against the British forces. Local farmers had reconnoitered the enemy positions, as well as movement of their cannons.

Accordingly, Stark assigned four units to surround the British encampment, with a plan to attack the forces simultaneously. Colonel Moses Nichols would man the right flank, heading east, and then north with two hundred of the New Hampshire volunteers. Colonel Samuel Herrick's Vermont Rangers

Reenactors at the British redoubt, Wilamoosac. *Courtesy of Norman Desmarais.*

would take the left flank, heading west and then north, to join Nichols's forces in an attack on the dragoon's redoubt on the hilltop. A third detachment under Hobart and Stickney would attack the Loyalist redoubts, while Stark and Warner would lead a direct assault on the central position at the trestle bridge crossing the Walloomsac River.

By midday, the rain had abated, and Stark ordered the men to move out and take their positions. As the flanking parties moved through the woods to take their positions, Stark and Warner rode onto the plain before the bridge and paraded their men before the watching Germans. When the German artillery began firing their cannons, Stark and his men fell back into camp and waited for the others to reach their positions.

At about 3:00 p.m., the signal firing of two muskets began the battle. The resultant exchange sounded, according to Stark, like "a continuous clap of thunder." The commander wrote to the Council of New Hampshire:

> *The action lasted two hours; at the expiration of which time we forced their breastworks, at the muzzle of their guns, took two pieces of brass cannon,*

with a number of prisoners; but before I could get them into proper form again, I received intelligence that there was a large reinforcement within two miles of us, on their march, which occasioned us to renew our attack; but luckily for us, Colonel Warner's regiment soon came up, which put a stop to their career. We soon rallied, and in a few minutes the action began very warm and desperate, which lasted until night. We used their cannon against them, which proved of great service to us.

At sunset we obliged them to retreat a second time; we pursued them till dark, when I was obliged to halt for fear of killing our men.[179]

Stark reported that he had lost 30 men in the battle, with another 42 wounded. The British suffered the deaths of 207 soldiers, with the majority of the remaining force either wounded or captured by the Americans. He praised the men under his command, whom, he wrote, fought "with the greatest spirit and bravery imaginable. Had they been Alexanders, or Charleses of Sweden, they could not have behaved better." He would echo these words in a letter to Congress several days after the battle, and by then, word of Stark's "singular victory" had spread through the states.

Stark's biographers pointed out that "[h]ad John Stark not defied General Lincoln at Manchester, only local militia would have stood in Baum's path. If Generals Schuyler and Lincoln disapproved of Stark's independent action,

Postcard of the monument at Bennington. *From the author's collection.*

and if his decisions annoyed Congress, at least one important observer… approved of Stark's strategy."[180]

General George Washington had written to Schuyler in late July, noting that having a body of dependable troops in the Grants territory would "keep him [Burgoyne] in continual anxiety for his rear…and would serve many other valuable purposes." He believed that if the British officer sent a detachment into the territory, it would be destroyed by American forces, and such a victory "would inspire the people and do away with their present anxiety. In such an event, they would loose sight of past misfortunes, and urged at the same time for regard for their own security, they would fly to Arms and afford every aid in their power."

Washington was correct in his prediction. As Stark and his men were marching the prisoners from Bennington to Boston, word came that the British had been defeated and abandoned Fort Stanwix in the western Mohawk Valley.

German general Friedrich Adolph von Riedesel would record that these back-to-back victories "raised the spirits of the enemy so amazingly, that the militias poured forth in crowds from the provinces of New Hampshire and New York."

John Stark would continue a distinguished career until his retirement in 1783. His greatest legacy was then, and still is, the Battle of Bennington— won entirely by militia and the cunning tactics of their leader.

Chapter 8

COLONEL JOHN BROWN, THE BERKSHIRE MEN AND THE BRITISH BURNING OF THE BREADBASKET IN THE MOHAWK RIVER VALLEY

Of the many men who served in the Revolutionary War and sacrificed their lives in states beyond their homeland, few had deeper connections to the region they would die defending than Colonel John Brown of Pittsfield, Massachusetts.

Brown was born in 1744, the son of Daniel Brown of Haverhill, Massachusetts. The family moved to the western part of the state when John was eight years old, settling in Sandisfield, a small community in Berkshire County tucked between the Farmington River Valley and Sandy Brook. John Brown's father soon became known as "Deacon Brown" in the village and took an active civic role in its affairs, an example that would influence his son immeasurably in the years to come.

Young John would enter Yale in 1767, a bit older than most students there, but he was remembered as a tall, athletic man on campus. He also studied prodigiously, as though to make up for lost time, and in the same vein, he got married before his graduation in 1771.[181]

While at college in New Haven, he had come to know Benedict Arnold, who had established himself in the merchant trade with the West Indies and Canada. He had a merchandise shop in town and lived on Water Street. Brown's sister, Elizabeth, had married Oliver Arnold, a brilliant lawyer who took Brown, as well as James Mitchell Varnum, under his tutelage. Oliver Arnold was the cousin of Benedict and served as the attorney general of Rhode Island until his untimely death in 1770 at the age of thirty-six.

The young John Brown doubtless knew of what some saw as Benedict Arnold's reputation in town for ignoring his creditors and taking to sea when they came by his shop looking for payment. He also likely had heard of Arnold's desertion from the British army, although in what view it was painted for him is unknown. He would come to take his own measure of Arnold some years later when their paths and swords crossed during the war.

After graduation, John Brown was admitted to practice law in Tryon County, New York. It was there, in the place where he began his adult life and where it would end in heroic tragedy less than a decade later, that Brown would have experienced firsthand the divisions that would fracture the citizens of the county when war with Great Britain erupted.

Sir William Johnson arrived in the Mohawk Valley in 1738 to assist his paternal uncle, Peter Warren, in establishing his estate. The young Johnson likely oversaw the Irish laborers recruited to build the house and outbuildings in that untamed country.

Johnson would found what is now known as Tryon County and would build a large stone mansion house and compound on the northern bank of the Mohawk River. He later built a second estate in present-day Johnstown called Johnson Hall.

Fort Johnson, Tryon County, New York. *Photo by the author.*

Johnson befriended the Mohawk tribe and learned their customs, cementing his bond by marrying a Mohawk woman of Iroquois royalty. In his later role as British superintendent of Indian affairs in North America, he would be instrumental in forging the "covenant chain" between the Iroquois Nation and Great Britain and remain a staunch defender of the Crown's right to rule in the colonies until the day he died.[182]

William Johnson's son, John Johnson, would inherit the compound as well as the elegant house in Johnstown, along with his father's fierce loyalty to the British Crown. The younger Johnson was placed in command of the local Loyalist militia and would spend much of the period before the war fighting the efforts of the established Committee of Safety and its actions to raise rebel militia in the county.

There is little to tell us of John Brown's political leanings when he began his practice in the county. He was successful and appointed the "King's Attorney" but also retained a close friendship with Yale classmate David Humphrey, who would later become Washington's private secretary. Perhaps Brown and his wife felt the Johnsons' influence too pervasive, for he resigned his position and they left in 1773 to settle in Pittsfield, Massachusetts.

John Brown and his law practice soon earned the respect of his new community, and in 1774, he was asked to compose the response of the Berkshire County's Committee of Correspondence to the events in Boston Harbor. While decrying the destruction of property by men disguised, after all, as Mohawk Indians, he empathized with their concerns about the reach and breadth of British law in the colonies and denounced the tyranny now practiced toward them by the Crown.

Brown was chosen to be a delegate to the General Court, the Assembly of the colony of Massachusetts. He was also chosen ensign of the local minutemen, and in February 1775, he led an armed party of men from Berskshire and Hampshire to Deerfield, where they arrested Tories suspected of having direct communication with British general Gage at Boston.

In March 1775, he was sent with a delegation to Montreal to meet with Canadians interested in aligning with the colonies in their dispute. While receiving support from merchant interests, he concluded that a consensus would never be reached in order to send delegates to the Continental Congress. Brown also recommended occupying Fort Ticonderoga in advance of any aggression by the Crown.[183]

His advice was taken, and a surprise attack on the Fort was executed on May 10, 1775, by troops, including the Pittsfield militia under command of Colonel James Easton. As a junior officer, Brown made an impression on commander Ethan Allen and challenged the authority declared by Benedict Arnold, a courageous stand for the young ensign.

The fort was, as we have seen, of strategic importance for the Americans, lying on Lake Champlain, which was a natural barrier between the thirteen colonies and British-controlled Canada. It also held a substantial amount of heavy armaments, including cannons and howitzers, within its walls.

Arnold, who knew the area of the fort well, had undertaken his own reconnaissance and reported his findings to Silas Deane's regiment in Connecticut, who passed the information to the Connecticut Committee of Correspondence. The committee acted at once, authorizing members to raise monies and recruit volunteers from western Massachusetts, Connecticut and the New Hampshire Grants territory.

It would come as little surprise, then, that a man such as Arnold, known for both his vanity and arrogance, would believe himself to be the rightful commander of such an expedition. But Arnold did not know of Brown's report to Massachusetts or of Ethan Allen's correspondence with members of the New Hampshire Grants, a territory that is now Vermont. He traveled to Boston in early May and informed the Massachusetts Committee of Safety of what he believed the fort contained in arms and that the structure presently held only a small garrison. The committee gave Arnold the authority to raise four hundred recruits for an attack, offering him £100 cash, horses, ammunition and gunpowder.

Arnold immediately set out with two captains appointed to help recruit the men needed. When they reached the border with Connecticut, they learned of the efforts there to recruit men for the same cause, and Arnold reputedly rode his horse to its death to reach Bennington the following day. Once there, he was informed that Allen was another fifty miles away and that the commander had already dispatched Samuel Herrick to Skenesboro and Asa Douglas to Panton with detachments to secure boats for the crossing. Arnold was also informed that Allen's men, known as the Green Mountain Boys, were not likely to acknowledge his command. The same was true of the Berskshire men.

Of the militia from Berkshire County, Brown's biographer wrote, "Berkshire took her part largely in her way when she sent men to fight the battles of the United Colonies. Her officers and men were often too independent to submit willingly to proper military authority, and in some trying emergencies the Berkshire men were insubordinate or were disposed to follow their leaders in attacks not always wisely chosen."

Allen had assembled one hundred of the Green Mountain Boys, and Brown, along with James Easton, had raised forty men from Pittsfield. Another twenty had joined them from Connecticut. In the dispute for command, John Brown sided with his men for Ethan Allen as commander. The two colonels met and came to an agreement. Historians differ as to whether it was a shared command, but the desired outcome was ultimately achieved.

Shortly before midnight on May 9, the forces assembled at Hand's Cove along the Vermont shoreline of Lake Champlain and waited for the boats needed to reach Ticonderoga. When they did arrive, around 1:30 a.m., there were not enough to adequately transport the troops. Eighty-three men made the first crossing with Allen and Arnold, and Asa Douglas was sent back to pick up the remainder.

Fearful that daylight might come before the men arrived, the two colonels made the decision to attack the fort with the force they had and subsequently marched to the south end of the fort, where the only sentry on duty misfired his musket and fled from the scene.

Detail of the Albany militia by Alan H. Archambault, plate no. 722, *Military Uniforms in America. From the author's collection.*

The Americans then easily stormed the fort, seizing weapons and gathering prisoners as they awoke. Allen and Arnold stormed the officers' quarters, and the British captain, realizing his predicament, had his assistant stall for time while he dressed himself for surrender.

John Brown was tasked by Ethan Allen with reporting the victory to the Continental Congress in Philadelphia, an honor of distinction for the young officer. Upon his return, Brown was appointed major of the Berkshire Regiment. That summer, following the victory at Ticonderoga, Major Brown was sent with four scouts into Canada to assess the conditions for a siege on the British forts in that wilderness.

Before the war, he could count on a number of French Canadians to shelter him or help with provisions during his travels. But now, as a spy, he could not risk putting them or his scouts in danger. At one point, the party was discovered and chased for miles. Despite these difficulties, Brown returned to Crown Point within a day of when he was scheduled to report to General Philip Schuyler.

Brown's advice was, again, that the Continental army should be proactive and make a foray into the northern country as soon as troops and supplies could be assembled. By August 1775, he had been placed in command of a flotilla on Lake Champlain.

As General Schuyler and Major General Richard Montgomery prepared the invasion of Quebec, they moved the Continental army into Isle de Noir on September 4. Plans were delayed when Schuyler became ill. The general penned a proclamation to the people of Quebec, urging them to assist the American cause. He then tasked Ethan Allen and John Brown to take a contingency of men and move north to disperse the proclamation and recruit soldiers to bolster the American attack. Schuyler then relinquished his command to Montgomery, and the general resumed the conquest with an attack on Fort Saint-Jean on September 18.

Allen and Brown had some success, meeting with sympathizer James Livingston at Chambly, who raised some three hundred men who encamped at Ponte-Olivier below the fort. British general Carleton had been forced to regroup his troops after the loss of Ticonderoga. He massed about five hundred of the eight hundred regular troops under his command at Fort Saint-Jean and sent the remaining regulars to man the smaller forts along the Great Lakes, as well as a small garrison at Montreal and another at Quebec City.

Carleton's attempt to raise recruits to bolster forces at the fort had been stymied by Wilkerson and other Patriot sympathizers, some of whom sent detailed information about British preparations to the American encampments. Nonetheless, by the time of the siege, he had amassed more than one hundred Canadian militia, twenty British Indian agents and a handful of indigenous allies to assist the small force of regulars from the Twenty-Sixth Foot that manned the garrison.

As the American siege began, Major General Montgomery ordered Ethan Allen to take thirty men and join Livingston's Canadian sympathizers and secure the southern bank of the St. Lawrence River, should the British send relief from Montreal. Montgomery also sent John Brown with his Berkshire men to secure the north and the road from Saint-Jean to Montreal.

Allen led a flotilla along the southern bank of the Richelieu River to Sorel, where he crossed and made his way up the St. Lawrence to Longuell. By Allen's account, he met Brown there, and the two determined to invade Montreal then and there. Brown with two hundred men would make the crossing at La Prairie, while Allen with his thirty men and some eighty Canadians under Livingston's captains would cross at Longuell. At a prearranged signal, the combined forces would attack the city.

It took three trips across the water to get Allen and his troops to the landing at Longue-Pointe. He posted men to prevent the inhabitants from informing the British of their presence and waited for Brown to arrive. The commander never brought his men across the river, but rather stayed where he had been ordered by Montgomery to secure the road.

When the alarm was raised at the British fort, Allen quickly maneuvered his men to a wooded area named Ruisseau de Soeurs and sent a scout to give word of their predicament to Thomas Walker, a merchant and known sympathizer. As the British force under Captain John Campbell made its way to Allen's hideout, the American commander ordered the Canadian troops to flank his right and left positions. These sympathizers fled within moments of the first shots being fired, and Allen and fifty men were forced to hold off the British forces. They held out for ninety minutes before being broken. Allen was run down and captured while trying to flee the enemy.

Ethan Allen's later narrative suggested that Brown's failure to comply with his plan had been the reason for the failure to capture Montreal and for his capture and subsequent imprisonment until he was exchanged in 1778. Brown never addressed the issue publicly as far as is known, but he did confront Allen personally after his release and rebuked him for his account.

Allen's plan was never approved by Generals Schuyler or Montgomery. In the aftermath of the failed expedition, Brown remained under General

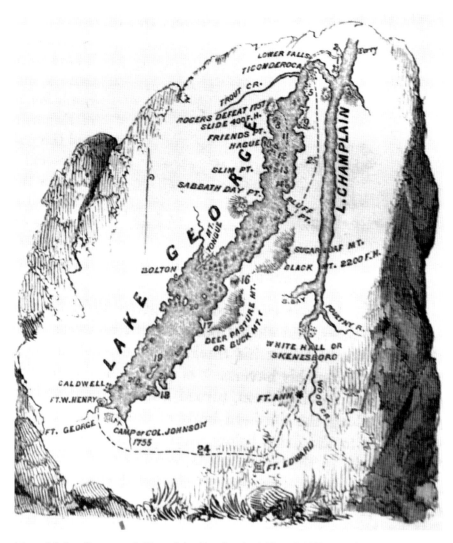

Map of Lakes George and Champlain. *From* Lossing's Pictorial History of the Revolutionary War.

Montgomery and, apparently, in his good graces. General Washington issued a statement that took Allen to task for his reckless behavior and noted that such behavior should be a caution to other junior officers and "teach a lesson of prudence and subordination to others who may be anxious to outshine their General officers."

On October 18, 1775, Brown was placed in charge of his Berkshire men along with James Livingston and his Canadian recruits to take Fort Chambly.

They gathered a force of some 350 men to lay siege. Fewer than 100 under British major John Stoppard protected the venerable fort.

Once the action began, the British soon discovered that they were far outnumbered. Oddly, they fired not one of the fort's cannons in defense and surrendered within forty-eight hours. The capture of the fort gave the Americans six tons of gunpowder and six thousand musket cartridges, as well as provisions, including 134 barrels of salted pork. The fall of Fort Chambly was key to the American success in the coming weeks, with Fort Saint-Jean finally surrendering by November 3 and the capture of Montreal ten days later. Later that month, Brown also forced the surrender of eleven British ships of sail, which now feared the battery the Americans possessed.

Writing of John Brown's leadership in the campaign, Major General Montgomery noted that "[u]pon this and all other occasions I have found him active and intelligent." Benedict Arnold, unsurprisingly, thought less of Brown and complained that he had let his men plunder the captured British vessels indiscriminately. But Arnold had few friends among the officers.

As winter set in, three of Arnold's junior officers, including Brown, formally asked to be placed under another command. Montgomery wrote with worry to Schuyler, though in the end, Brown stayed put, even as the majority of his men went home after the capture of Montreal; he was placed in command of a small number that remained. He and Montgomery would then join Arnold in the Siege of Quebec.

Montgomery arrived at Port Au Trembles with three hundred men from the First, Second and Third New York Regiments and a company of artillery led by John Lamb. With the general were Brown and 160 men

Illustration of the Mohawk Valley breadbasket. *From* Lossing's Pictorial History of the Revolutionary War.

who remained of the Berkshire men, many of whom had gone home after their term of service expired, as well as Livingston and 200 of his Canadian recruits. They also brought provisions and clothing plundered from the British ships for Arnold's men, many of whom were nearly starved and destitute of clothes. Weary of Arnold's disregard for their welfare, a number of captains requested that Montgomery place them under his command.

Despite the apparent turmoil within the gathered forces, the plan for an attack proceeded, and the Americans lay siege to the city on December 6. Montgomery sent a letter to the British commander demanding his surrender. General Carleton reputedly burned the letter unread. A second attempt by Montgomery elicited no response. The five mortars he had brought to besiege the city soon began firing at the massive walls, but with little effect. When British cannons destroyed two of the guns, Montgomery was forced to withdraw the remaining mortars. On December 10, the Americans attempted to entrench their larger artillery within seven hundred yards of the fort. As the ground was too frozen to dig trenches, the artillery improvised by building a wall made from blocks of snow, behind which they could rest their guns.

This also proved ineffective, and the general soon realized that he was in peril of losing the battle before it had even begun. The vast majority of troops from New York would see their own terms of service expire on December 31. Despite pleas for them to enlist for another few weeks, it became clear that they were frustrated by the lack of food, clothing and the very real danger of being killed or taken prisoner; this would diminish the troops even further if action were not taken soon.

A snowstorm on December 27 gave Montgomery the cover he needed to move his men into place, and he quickly prepared for attack. The storm subsided, however, and his plans for the time were foiled. They were also placed in danger from a British deserter named John Hall, who went back into the city and informed Carleton of Montgomery's plan.

Undaunted, the American general drew up another plan of attack. Brown's role in the siege was now to take Livingston and lead a combined force of Americans and Canadians in a diversionary attack on the western walls of the Upper Town of the city, while Arnold and Montgomery's forces attacked the Lower Town from two directions.

On the afternoon of December 30, a northeaster arrived, bringing fierce winds and heavy snow. Montgomery ordered his men to assemble for the attack. Brown led his men with Livingston to their positions that night. When he reached the western walls between four o'clock and five o'clock in the morning, he shot off a pair of flares to let Arnold and Montgomery know that they had arrived.

In the snow and ice, Montgomery led his force down a steep ravine toward the lower walls. When they reached the outer defenses, carpenters had to saw through the palisades the British had erected. When a second palisade was finally breached, the general unsheathed his sword and led an advance party of fifty men into the town. As they made their way toward a two-story blockade at the end of the street, gunfire erupted from inside and Montgomery was killed instantly, with many around him also killed or wounded. The remaining members of the party retreated to the palisades.

Carleton, meanwhile, had learned of the attempted attack by Arnold at Porte Palais, and the diversion led by Brown and Livingston was exposed. The commander quickly rallied some five hundred troops comprising sailors and Royal Highlanders to move on Lower Town. These men, under Captain George Laws, retook the barricade that Morgan's riflemen had breached, thereby trapping them within the city.

In the aftermath of the defeat, Arnold and the remaining forces hunkered down to continue the siege. It was a difficult winter, with smallpox ravaging the encampment and the troops further diminished by those who refused to reenlist and set out for home. In March 1776, Brown wrote to his wife that Arnold had given him orders to "to attack with his attachment of 200 men, one half of whom were sick in the hospital." Brown obeyed orders and marched out what able-bodied men he could muster, only to find the enemy had already retired within their fort.

Such was his outrage at Arnold's seeming disregard for the men that Brown complained in December 1776 to Major General Horatio Gates, including a charge that during the Battle of Ticonderoga, Arnold had to be arrested to prevent him from deserting to the British. These concerns were passed along to Congress, but Arnold's star was still bright in the eyes of those officers and congressmen far removed from the plight of the men sent into battle.

Believing that his complaints had fallen on deaf ears, Brown composed and printed a handbill that winter of 1776–77 that spelled out what he believed were the general's faults in leadership and character: "Money is this man's God, and to get enough of it he would sacrifice his country."

Such clear insubordination would have meant the end of the military career of a junior officer. But charges for court-martial were never brought against Brown, although the Congress did decline to give Arnold the promotion he desired. It was perhaps advantageous for his career that

Illustration of a Continental soldier in the Canadian campaign by Allan H. Archambault.
Courtesy of the Rhode Island Society of the Sons of the American Revolution.

when Arnold returned on April 1 after recovering from the leg wound he received in Quebec, he fell off his horse almost immediately and had to return to Montreal.

Brown himself was an adept horseman. There is evidence that among the Berkshire men were mounted soldiers. They were certainly in use at the battle of what may be the most esteemed moment of Brown's military career, his successful raid on Fort Ticonderoga.

Militia throughout New England had maintained horses both draught and riding stallions for mobility. As with other regions, some part of the Berkshire County militia mustered mounted, while most were equipped as foot soldiers who could also ride when they needed to move quickly over the rugged terrain.[184]

In the waning months of the summer of 1777, General Benjamin Lincoln called out to the Berkshire militia for another enlistment. He needed men and horses, calling on the county "for a body of their militia…mounted, each bringing their sack of flour."

John Brown had now become colonel of the Berkshire militia and organized its arrival at Lincoln's encampment for September 12. Colonel Brown chose his men carefully for the coming raid. There were a considerable number of Vermonters—some no doubt were veterans whom Brown knew well. Some of these men may have been mounted as well. Brown's raid was one of three simultaneous attacks orchestrated by General Lincoln. Historians also commend the wide range of Brown's attack and the quickness of the raids along the way to the fort.

Brown's route was to trace the southern bank of Lake Champlain to a fording place called "The Narrows." Once across, the party made its way along the rugged hillsides between Lake Champlain and Lake George, until descending on the fort on the morning of September 18, 1777.

One young man named Jacob Bayley penned his enthusiastic account of the raids:

> [A]*t day-break Col. Brown began ye attack, set at liberty 100 of our men which were prisoners; took prisoners 293 of the enemy, amongst which were Capts., 7 Lieuts., and two other officers. Took Mount Defiance, Mount Hope, the French lines and Blockhouse at the landing, 200 Battaus, one armed sloop, several gun-boats. On Sunday took about 100 prisoners… took a vast quantity of plunder….Col. Brown is now reinforced now to 700. We mean to keep possession of the ground at Ticonderoga, the field is now open wide, the time is now come* [that] *we may intirely cut off*

Reenactors inside Fort Ticonderoga. *Courtesy of Norman Desmarais.*

General Burgoyne's whole army if we exert ourselves....I think it the Duty of every man to turn out with his horse & one month's provisions; which will undoubtedly accomplish our design. I must call on all Friends to America to turn out & come to our assistance in Ticonderoga.[185]

Colonel John Brown resigned his commission and returned to Pittsfield. He was appointed to serve as a judge in 1779. And he remained there, as commander of the Berkshire militia, until called up again in the summer of 1780.

JOHN JOHNSON HAD LONG been waiting for his revenge. He had suffered the humiliating raid on Fort Johnson, now a resplendent English-style estate with a circular drive and formal gardens. The heir of the Johnson legacy had dismantled the old fort of its outbuildings, expanded the use of the grounds to gardening and upgraded to an elegant, French-roofed privy.

Less than a month after the death of Sir William Johnson on July 11, 1774, the Tryon County Committee of Safety gathered at Louck's Tavern in Stone Arabia to draft its response to the British blockade of Boston. The committee resolved to respond forcefully, and like those brave men who drafted such correspondence in other colonies, they faced being accused of treason for expressing their convictions. The committee from Tryon County was mindful of the divisions within its community and sent a delegation to Johnson's home to inform him and his Iroquois allies that their fight was not with them, but the British Crown.

Johnson may have feigned humility and perhaps relief to the delegation, but he had not been idle in keeping his militia trained and provided with weapons. Eventually, he was found out, and General Philip Schuyler was given two thousand troops to convince Johnson to surrender his men and the arms he had accumulated. As the raid apparently took Johnson by surprise, he and three hundred supporters had no choice but to surrender.

Still, knowing Sir Johnson's standing in the community, Schuyler thought it prudent to negotiate a peaceful solution to the Loyalists' activities. He received a false promise of neutrality from Johnson and left him on parole. It was a decision that was to have dire consequences for the citizens of Mohawk Valley.

In early May 1780, information was received that Johnson was moving with a large force from Lake Champlain and marching for Johnstown. At the same time, Mohawk leader Joseph Brandt and the Iroquois were rumored to be roaming through the Canajoharie territory, destroying everything in their path, and planned to meet with the Loyalist troops before the presumed raid on the valley. If this was indeed the plan, Johnson did not wait for his indigenous allies to act.

ON THE TWENTY-FIRST, SIR John Johnson and his forces landed at Bulwagga Bay, close to Crown Point, and from there began a march of destruction. Once reaching Tribes Hill, they "plundered, murdered, and destroyed every farm and settlement within a ten-mile stretch along the valley." Every man they came across capable of bearing arms was executed. As the carnage came to a close, Johnson and his men left the smoldering ruins of houses and fields behind and were finally chased from the valley by local militia.

On June 22, the General Court of Massachusetts directed that some 4,726 men should be raised, per General Washington's request that drafts be made of the local militia or volunteers be enlisted for three months' service in New York State. These levies, as they would be called, some 702 from Berkshire County alone, would be sent to areas needed to support the Continental

Illustration of New York provincial forces by Alan H. Archambault, plate no. 657, *Military Uniforms in America. From the author's collection.*

Fort Frey, one of the "stone forts" dotting the Mohawk Valley that date from the time of the French and Indian War. *Photo by the author.*

troops; 315 men from the Berkshire brigade were sent to Tiverton, Rhode Island, and served there under General Heath. Another 387 men were sent to the Mohawk Valley and dispersed among the various forts, whose populations shifted over the months and into fall, as troops moved between the large defenses of Fort Plain and Fort Plank to the older and less protected stone "forts" that dotted the Mohawk Valley.

That summer of 1780, the citizens of the Mohawk Valley knew that the danger was near and present. The valley had been supplying grain to the rebel troops since the outbreak of the war and had come to be known as the "breadbasket" of the American army. The importance of the Mohawk River had been established since the French and Indian War, when stone houses, some with fortified enclosures, had been erected along the banks of the river and throughout the Mohawk Valley.

Constructed as blockhouses for citizens' safety, a number would be expanded in the Revolutionary War and used for defense. Others were newly constructed on a more expansive plan. Fort Paris was one such defense. Built in 1777, the fort was constructed around the 1737 Paris farmhouse and outbuildings. All was enclosed with a palisade fence and included a blockhouse and a barrack that could house one hundred men.[186]

Brown would officially take command of his brigade on July 14, 1780. Of the approximately 380 men under his command, only 217 men of his Berkshire regiment would be with him at Fort Paris. Major Oliver Root was second in command. The remainder of his troops comprised a detachment of the First Regiment of Tyron County under Captain Joyst Dygert, a large body of local militia from the Second Regiment of Tyron County under Captain Henry Miller and a detachment of Tyron County Rangers under Captain John Kasselman.

Mohawk Joseph Brant had delayed his attack until July. That month, he sent a small force to conduct a feint attack on Fort Schuyler, drawing General Robert Van Rensselaer away from his post at Stone Arabia, a plateau between Garoga Creek and Johnstown, north of the Mohawk River. Brant then used the diversion to lay waste to the Canajoharie settlements a second time. Troops who had been sent from Albany to protect the citizens proved inefficient.

On September 7, the New York Assembly authorized Governor Clinton to order out whatever number of militia he thought sufficient to protect the state's citizens. Brigadier General James Clinton was assigned command at Albany, and Generals Ten Broek and Van Rensselaer were to provide any needed support.

Johnson's forces continued to march through the countryside seemingly at will, making their way along the Oswego River and Oneida Lake and across country to the Susquehanna Valley, where they raided settlements and briefly laid siege to Middle Fort. Turning north, they raided the entirety of the country to Fort Hunter. By the evening of October 18, Johnson and his forces were encamped at the Nose on the south side of the Mohawk River, just miles from where Brown waited for word at Fort Paris.

General Van Rensselaer had arrived at Caughnawaga to find the community in flames. He also learned that Johnson was marching to Stone Arabia and dispatched messages to Colonel Lewis Dubois at Fort Plain and to Brown at Fort Paris to move out in the morning and engage the enemy. He planned to arrive with his forces in time to drive the Loyalists back after the American troops stalled Johnson's progress. As with many best-laid plans, circumstances caused the events of the battle to go far differently, and Rensselaer would be denied his imagined victory.

The circumstances that led to the American defeat are shrouded in some mystery. While there is every indication that the correct communication was received at Fort Plain, there is some question as to the message that came to Colonel Brown at Fort Paris. Private William Feeter recalled that

"Col. Brown…received orders from Genl. Van Rensselaer who was coming up the river from Schenectady, to give the enemy battle, & he would attack them in the rear."

A few historians have written that Brown and his men were led into an ambush by a "deserter" who had somehow managed to convince Colonel Brown and Major Root that his information on the location and number of Johnson's forces could be trusted. Johnson himself believed this was the cause of Brown's leaving the fort. In his report after the battle, he stated that "two men who had deserted from Fort Stanwix this spring left us and went over to the enemy at Stone Arabia and informed Colonel Brown, who commanded there, that the Detachment on that side of the River was very weak, which induced him the next morning with three Hundred and sixty men to attack him."[187]

Or was the man who delivered the orders to Brown an imposter, as indicated in more than one soldier's recollection?

Andrew Yew, one of the Massachusetts men, recalled, "The pretended bearer of Orders rode beside Col. Brown at the head of the regiment and led us into an ambush. We were suddenly fired upon from the front & both sides & a great many killed."

Howe recounted that Van Rensselaer "sent a messenger with a letter to Col. Brown, and another to Colonel Dubois at Fort Plain, telling Brown to march at dawn the next day to delay the enemy and to expect reinforcements. "Furthermore," Howe explained, "it is said that Brown's officers and men advised him to disobey the order, as it was not the time to leave the Fort."

Indeed, Colonel Dubois had urged Brown to withdraw from Stone Arabia to the large fort that occupied the long plateau at Fort Plain. However, Howe also alluded to some deception that led to the fatal encounter: "[B]eing deceived by the false advice of persons pretending to be patriots, he was led to turn aside from the road upon which he marched out into a somewhat narrow clearing in the forest near a small work called Fort Keyser, and was killed nearly two miles from Fort Paris."

FORT PLAIN BLOCK-HOUSE.¹

Illustration of the blockhouse at Fort Plain, New York. *From* Lossing's Pictorial History of the Revolutionary War.

This would seem to indicate that a number of persons intercepted Brown and his men and convinced them to turn off the road to pursue a body of the enemy. This is also quite different from the charge of a false messenger or "pretended bearer of orders."

To further complicate the scene, Brown's biographer, Garret L. Roof, introduced another diversion that he described as the prelude to the assault, after the troops had passed Fort Keyser: "After they had proceeded a short distance further, one of Colonel Brown's volunteers discovered an Indian… pursuing two women as they were running from their homes. The Indian discharged his musket at one of the women. The woman fell, and as he ran to scalp her, the fire of the brave volunteer brought the savage to the earth. A destructive fire was then opened upon the soldiers of Brown."[188]

Roof's description of "wily Indians" is based on an "eyewitness" account from a man in the rear guard of Brown's column. So far removed from the scene was he that he wrote in his pension application that the fallen colonel had already been hastily buried by the time he and his fellow soldiers had reached the site. Historian James F. Morrison found widely differing accounts from the survivors' pension applications, at least one written as late as fifty-six years after the battle. It is not difficult to imagine that the memory of events and specifics of a battle might be muddied over the years, and perhaps the retreat of the advance guard under Major Oliver Root to the main body was so sudden and unexpected that an ambush would have been a logical conclusion. But Roof, the biographer, used these "eyewitness accounts," and along with other details—like that of Colonel Brown on his black horse, being "shot through the heart by a musket ball from the enemy and fell lifeless to the earth"—this suggests that his account is penned for an audience he assumed would be moved more by sensationalism. His description of the scalping and defilement of Brown's body is especially grisly, especially if one pauses to remember that the words were spoken before a gathering of what must have been considered some of the more refined members of Oneida County in 1884.

Today, the greater consensus is that Colonel Brown followed orders, and his regiment was simply overwhelmed by the combined forces of Johnson's men and Brant's warriors long before reinforcements arrived.

William Feeter recalled in his pension application, "[Colonel] Brown marched out of the fort & attacked the enemy. [Feeter] & other militia of the Stone Arabia joined Brown & were in the battle. Brown fell fighting manfully & about thirty or forty of his men were also killed& the remainder retreated."[189]

Site of the battlefield at Stone Arabia, New York. *Photo by the author.*

Historians Foote and Storm presented the battle in just this way:

> *The rebels were enveloped on both their flanks and assaulted on their front.
> The American line soon crumbled and the remnants of the shattered troops
> fled in disorder. A few may have concealed themselves in the woods, many
> found refuge in nearby fortified homesteads. Several…were pursued, some
> to be run down and killed, including six who sought refuge behind a large
> boulder. More than thirty men were left dead on the field, including the
> courageous Brown…as he rode his lines directing his troops.*[190]

Later historians would lean toward the conclusion that Brown acted on
orders and that the Loyalist and rebel troops simply met as they marched
and the resulting skirmish resulted in Brown's death. Canadian historian
Gavin K. Watts pointed out that "so many American historians search
for an answer to Brown's defeat by turning to explanations of treachery
on the part of "patriots" and carefully laid ambushes on the part of
Indians."[191]

But Watt aptly pointed out that two missives were found in Brown's pocket by Johnson when he arrived at the site. One was an update on Colonel Van Rensselaer's progress on reaching Fort Hunter with "six hundred militia and three field pieces," indicating that he was close by, and the other was the note from Dubois informing Brown that he expected "to March the rest of the troops by break of Day" and added, "You will inform me with all the Enemies movement." This would seem to indicate that Brown acted on these letters and marched the troops out, expecting to align with forces dispatched by Dubois.

Watt's modern account dismissed any speculation about an ambush and concluded that the advanced guard, having turned up the narrow path up the deep ravine through which Homestead Creek flowed, simply collided head-on with Brant's men, who drove the Massachusetts militia back toward Brown's main body of troops. Watt's wrote that "Brown's main body had taken position in a woods behind a stone fence which bordered the roadway. It was not an ideal defensive position as it lay in a hollow. The far side of the road was also lined by a stone fence with open fields beyond it."[192]

It was through these open fields that Johnson's men followed Brandt's advance, and as they came upon the rebels' position "a brisk skirmish commenced in which Colonel Brown, who was prominent atop his black horse was killed. His death occurred on the exact day of his thirty-sixth birthday."

In the aftermath of the colonel's fall, his men disbanded, and "the routed rebels either fled towards the Stone Arabia forts or took to the woods, heading south towards the Mohawk River. Both groups were pursued and some were run down and killed."[193]

After this initial attack came a running battle that swept the breadth of Stone Arabia from eastward to the southeast. Van Rensselaer's men caught up with Johnson's forces in late afternoon after crossing the river at Fort Plain. Johnson had swept southward after the destruction at Stone Arabia, intending to lay waste to the settlements along the Mohawk River. It was there, however, that his men encountered the series of stone forts and were forced to "[t]ake to the woods and avoid three of four fortified houses that entirely commanded the roads & flats."[194]

By the time Van Rensselaer engaged Johnson's men, they had reached the farm of Colonel Jacob Klock, and as the light began to wane, the battle unfolded at Klock's field.

With such a scarcity of primary sources, historians have had to piece together what they can of the details of the battle. A few facts emerge that

Site of "Klock's Field," Stone Arabia, New York. *Photo by the author.*

indicate that Van Rensselaer's confidence was misguided and that it was a far greater struggle for the Americans to repel such an invasion from within.

Dubois brought his forces to the height on the north side of Johnson's forces. Lieutenant Colonel John Harper and his sixty Oneida volunteers took a position on the south side, with Van Rensselaer's troops.

When Johnson's Loyalist forces emerged from the woods, the militia on the left flank reportedly responded "in great disorder." They could initially offer only sporadic fire, fell back and then surged forward again. As the battle lines moved back and forth across the field, Van Rensselaer's men gained advantage, only to be undermined by the poor positioning of the troops meant to cover their forward movement. The general's aide-de-camp wrote, "The troops in the low ground had commenced in firing at a long shot from the enemy, broke, and some ran."[195] This forced Van Rensselaer's forces to draw back some three miles downriver before regaining some momentum.

The tide turned when the allied Iroquois fell back as a large force of rebels drew close to their position and then withdrew across the Mohawk River. The action emboldened Van Rensselaer's men, and some seized the opportunity to push their companies forward. They fired briskly on Johnson's forces, who soon brought up reinforcements from the British Thirty-Fourth Regiment of Foot, as well as the Royal Yorkers, but these in the end could not sway what was now the rebel advantage in the field.

As darkness fell, the threat of friendly fire caused Van Rensselaer to halt his troops' pursuit of the Loyalists. He ordered them back to Colonel Klock's house, where they could get victuals and some much-needed rest—most had gotten little sleep since Johnson withdrew his forces across the river—and the long day of destruction had ended.

All the men who had died in that early battle were buried in a mass grave. A few days later, Colonel John Brown's body was disinterred and brought to a burial site about three hundred yards west of the Reformed Dutch Church in Stone Arabia. There he was laid to rest in what must have been a somber ceremony, attended by the depleted members of his regiment, with others who had survived the onslaught, although "everything but the soil" around them had been destroyed. Johnson's burning of the breadbasket had decimated a swath of some twenty-three miles of the Mohawk River Valley.

On October 19, 1836, a small crowd gathered to dedicate a monument at the site of his burial. Among them was the colonel's son, Henry Brown, then a sheriff in his home of Berkshire County. A sermon and then a historical address were delivered by Reverend Abraham N. Van Horne. The description on the granite monument reads simply

> *In Memory of Col. John Brown*
> *Who was Killed in Battle on the 19th day of October, 1780,*
> *At Palatine, in the County of Montgomery.*
> *Aged 36*

Colonel John Brown, like many of the Berkshire men, died far from home, willingly defending the idea of liberty in a place of strangers. Leaders like Brown gave voice to the men who had enlisted in their fervent call to rally for freedom. They displayed their own character and were an example to their men. As Brown and others understood, such character was key in gaining respect from the men under your command.

In another memorial address on Colonel John Brown delivered by Archibald Murray Howe before the Palatine Historical Society in 1908, concern was expressed for the neglected state of the monument and perhaps, as well, what Howe perceived as the fading memory of Brown's heroic death.

Monument at Fort Plain, New York. *Photo by the author.*

More than a century later, the memorial remains well preserved, and Brown's memory, though long faded but for a plaque in his home of Pittsfield, remains very much as a hero to the historians and their fellow citizens of Mohawk County.

Those brave leaders and the equally brave men who followed them brought liberty to every town and village across the landscape of the thirteen colonies. Though differing in origin and customs and, at times in dialect and devotion, the citizen soldiers who gathered from far and wide shared the same dream of an America united in its hope for freedom and prosperity—not only for oneself but also for one's neighbors and fellow countrymen.

INDEPENDENCE AFTER WAR

The independence of spirit within militia units, as well as the public regard for them, continued during the entirety of the war and well after the conflict with Great Britain had ended. Despite the difficulties extant with the militias' relationship with the Congress and Continental army, Washington and other Revolutionary leaders had "heralded that heritage, and wanted the army to respect it and in doing so to be not only an instrument but a model for the new American Republic."

The historian Don Higginbotham summarized the efforts of Congress to utilize the militia during the war: "As an institution…the militia proved deficient. The law-making bodies of the colony-states were never able to bring these military [units] up to meeting their responsibilities. The reason in part is that, as time passed, those responsibilities were vastly enlarged—to the point of embracing everything of a military nature. If we are mindful of this all-encompassing role they were asked to play, then we can better understand their limits and their failures."[196]

On June 2, 1784, Congress reissued the disbandment order of the Continental army under the principle that "standing armies in time of peace are inconsistent with the principles of republican government, dangerous to the liberties of a free people, and generally converted into destructive engines for establishing despotism." But one founder in particular was headstrong in his efforts to wrangle the glory of the Revolution into establishing a standing federal army that would be overseen by the new government and guided by a host of rules and regulations that Alexander Hamilton had been scribbling for posterity during the closing campaigns of the war.

This founder had an ally during the war in General Nathanael Greene, who as early as 1775 had written that "all the force in America should be under one Commander raised and appointed by the same Authority; subjected to the same Regulations and ready to be detach where ever Occasion may require."[197]

But it was not to be. Americans again refused to embrace the idea of a federal army that would supersede their own community militia. The "Regular Army," as it became known, was the First American Regiment, established in 1784, and later named the Regiment of Infantry, and after its first posting to Fort Mcintosh in Western Pennsylvania, it was dispatched to the western frontier.

Historian Edward M. Coffman described the struggles that attempts to raise a standing army, separate and independent of militia, faced during that period: "During the three decades after the War for Independence, The American army struggled into existence. Despised and feared by many, it waxed and waned in response to the Indian Wars and the rumors of invasion threats. From 1783–1788 the weak Confederation Congress maintained it on an ad hoc basis at a strength never more than 700 men."[198]

As late as 1795, British traveler Isaac Weld wrote incredulously of what had become of the army that had earned America its independence. Visiting a fort on the United States side of Niagara, he observed that while the French had built the garrison to hold five hundred men, "The federal garrison…consists of fifty men; and the whole of the cannon in the place amounts merely to four small field pieces, planted at the four corners of the fort."

Worse still was the condition and lack of discipline displayed by the soldiers, as "the greater part of the men were as dirty as if they had been at work in the trenches for a week without intermission: their grizzly beards demonstrated that a razor had not approached their chins for many days; their hair, to appearance, had not been combed for the same length of time; their linen was filthy, their guns rusty, and their clothes ragged."[199]

As there was little support among constituents, Congress also showed little support for the standing army. They were poorly supplied, poorly paid and had little training or discipline. Any community would have gladly stood the men who lived within their towns or villages up against what was then called the American army. There were no longer minutemen to raise on an alarm, but there were many veterans who returned and led local militias, and these units remained the preferred defense of many Americans.

Those militias continued to raise protests, especially when it came to the laxity of Congress in honoring pensions and addressing the issue of what we would now call veterans' benefits. Those protests that would become well known included the Pennsylvania Line "mutinies" of 1781 and 1783, the first a daring act of rebellion that nearly included a march on Congress but was negotiated to a peaceful settlement within the week of breaking out. The second occurred after the war and addressed the same issues of pay and better housing. Eighty men of the Lancaster militia, who helped guard the barracks and ammunition depot, joined the former Continental soldiers in Philadelphia.

The protest began on June 17 when a letter demanding payment for their service in the war was sent by the Philadelphia Continentals to Congress, with the threat of taking action if their demands were not met. Congress initially ignored the letter, but by June 20, after the arrival of the Lancaster militia, a mob of some four hundred soldiers occupied the statehouse and barred members of Congress from leaving until Alexander Hamilton assured the leaders of the rebellion that Congress would address the issue. Of course, once the members were allowed to leave, they did no such thing. They met in secret and drafted a letter to the Pennsylvania Council asking for protection from the mutineers.

The council refused the request, believing that local militia called on to quell the disturbance would not fire on their former comrades. The rebellion continued then unabated until Washington sent 1,500 troops to Philadelphia, a number of the leaders were arrested and the remaining troops dispersed.

Perhaps because so many veterans were involved, the response of the government to the Pennsylvania rebellions was relatively tame. A similar action led by a New Jersey militia at the close of the war resulted in the executions of the leaders of the mutinies.

A less remembered incident today was a protest that resulted in the court-martial of Captain Samuel Watson and several other men of the First Regiment, First Brigade, Seventh Division, of the Massachusetts militia in 1810.

The charge against Watson and the others was insubordination in that they purposely had failed to bring the men under their command to a called muster in Worcester, Massachusetts, in the spring of 1810 due to the location not being central to those communities' militia. In failing to appear, and in Watson's case purportedly encouraging those other militia officers to be absent as well, he was effectively refusing to follow his commander's orders.

In his opening remarks in defense of his actions, Watson stated:

I shall endeavor in the first place, to shew that Worcester South Meeting House is far from the centre of the Regiment, and also from the centre of the troops composing the Regiment. I shall in the next place, make it appear, that in Colonel Brigham's opinion, the Regiment ought never to be paraded in Worcester, because it was uncentral and discommoded the men, and then shew the reasons which Colonel Brigham assigned for not meeting in the centre, and the inducements he had for coming to Worcester. And lastly, shall shew that near the centre there is [as] good a parade ground as in Worcester.[200]

But this was mostly smoke and mirrors. Watson's protest was really about a change in the law that the Commonwealth had instituted just weeks before the call to muster, one that effectively stripped him and other militia commanders of their say as to where the men would muster.

After establishing once again that he had proven the meetinghouse at Leicester to be the central location for mustering his men, Watson argued against the newly established law, harkening back to the former statute from 1793 that stated that "every Regiment of Militia in this Commonwealth shall be assembled in Regiments once in two years for Review, Inspection, and Discipline, on such days as the Commanding officers of the several Divisions or Brigades should order—the Commanding Officers of the Regiments to point out the place…and the places to be appointed for review of inspection as aforesaid shall always be as central as in the judgment of the Officer pointing out the place."

In addition, the old statute contained the clause that "no Officer or non-commissioned soldier shall be obliged to march a greater distance than fifteen miles from home to any Brigade review." As these regulations were presently under review, they remained in place; therefore, as the location ordered by Colonel Brigham turned out to be more than fifteen miles from several communities whose men made up the regiment, the colonel's order then was illegal, and the soldiers in turn were not bound to follow those orders.

Watson argued, "If troops were bound to obey the illegal orders of the superior officers, a Military Despotism would be established in this Country, such as never disgraced the annals of the most barbarous despot. The property, liberty and lives of our Fellow-Citizens would be jeopardized upon the altar of relentless tyranny, and the will of an unprincipled officer would become the scourge of a miserable people."

In the court decision, Watson was found guilty of disobeying orders but not guilty of insubordination or of aiding and abetting other officers in their neglect of duty. He was removed from his command and barred from military service for one year. Each of his fellow defendants put forward the same argument. Captain David Livermore told the court, "During the whole course of my life, from sixteen years old, to the present time, I have been compelled to march from my own town to Regimental musters, and often further from the centre than from Spencer to the centre. Eight years I have been under the disagreeable necessity of giving orders to my company to the same effect. This I considered an evil, but an evil I had no right to oppose....I patiently endured it, hoping and expecting redress of grievances by the Legislature."[201]

But clearly those in the present government did not meet his expectations, and he railed against what he saw as the foreshadowing of "an unlimited monarchy":

> *If the doctrine of* non-resistance *and* passive obedience *is to be established, I must meet the reward of my temerity. Although I do not believe...the people yet base and blinded enough to advocate a principal so destructive to our liberty, independence, and forms of Republican Government....Establish it by your decision, and you say we are no longer worthy the name of Freemen. Our Courts of Justice may be abolished and our forms of Government* lit up as a taper *to usher us into eternal darkness. Then may we emphatically say, as has been predicted, "The glory of America has passed away."*[202]

Captain Livermore received an identical sentence from the court, as did Captain Daniel Kent. Only Captain William Prouty was found not guilty of any charges filed against him.

While the Commonwealth may have won these small battles, the long-held distrust of a standing army remained. Even up until the time of the Civil War, the regular army remained small and had spent much of the preceding forty-five years routing indigenous tribes from territory newly acquired or desired by the United States government.

In 1903, Secretary of State Elihu Root attempted to reform the United States military. The passage of the Militia Act that year included the key provision that state militias would receive federal funding and equipment in exchange for adhering to federal standards of training and organizing. Those state militias that ceded their organization to the federal government would be called the National Guard.

In Rhode Island, the state militia was officially re-designated as the Rhode Island National Guard by General Order No. 9 on April 15, 1907. The two

Monument to the unknown fallen soldiers at Saratoga, New York. *Photo by the author.*

infantry regiments of the brigade of Rhode Island militia were reorganized as coast artillery companies in order to provide a trained reserve of soldiers to man the five coastal defense forts in Rhode Island. Other units were a cavalry squadron and a light artillery battery.

A few of the chartered units of the Rhode Island militia chose not to convert to National Guard units. This was mostly because they would be denied the privilege of electing their own officers. These units included the Artillery Company of Newport, Bristol Train of Artillery, the Kentish Guards and the Pawtuxet Rangers. These units, along with several others, today comprise the Historic Military Commands of the Rhode Island Militia.[203]

It was not until 1917 that a national army made up of conscripted men and volunteer enlistees was established by the Department of War.

NOTES

Preface

1. Higginbotham, *War of American Independence*, 205–6.
2. Ibid., 177.

Chapter 1

3. Bell, *Road to Concord*, 23.
4. Wright, *Massachusetts Militia Roots.*
5. Ibid.
6. Bell, *Road to Concord*, 65.
7. Raphael, "Country Crowds in Revolutionary Massachusetts," 2.
8. Ibid., 3.
9. Robertson, "Decoding Connecticut Militia," 4.
10. Ibid., 8.
11. Sylvanus diary.
12. Robertson, "Decoding Connecticut Militia," 8.
13. Ibid., 8.
14. Goodrich, *Rolls of the Soldiers*, 2–13.
15. Smith, *Civil and Military List of Rhode Island*, 6.
16. A general order sent out by the colony's Assembly in May 1673 stated, "In war with the Dutch, none may be compelled to trayne or fight against

their conscience, but shall be required to watch and inform of danger, and to perform civill service."

17. Smith, *Civil and Military List of Rhode Island*, 22.

18. Sheryka, *Four Documents in the History of the Kentish Guard*.

19. Christopher Greene served as lieutenant in the Kentish Guard at the time of the Lexington alarm when the unit marched to Boston. He was appointed major with the formation of Varnum's Brigade and volunteered for the expedition under Benedict Arnold to Quebec, where he was captured and held captive until August 1777. Upon his release, Greene was appointed by General Washington as colonel of the First Rhode Island Regiment. He would show great skill at outmaneuvering the enemy when the regiment was sent to defend Fort Mercer at Red Bank, New Jersey, and his men displayed great loyalty. Many of these men would become part of the Second Rhode Island Regiment, and the newly formed First Rhode Island, under the plan promoted by General James Mitchell Varnum and approved by Washington in 1778, was to be formed entirely of slaves who enlisted to earn their freedom. The First Rhode Island would ultimately be an amalgamation of former slaves, free men of color, a handful of indentured servants of European background and poor farm boys seeking adventure, or at least some pay for their labors. Greene would effectively train the unit, which played a key role in the Battle of Rhode Island in August 1778, but he was later killed in a surprise attack from a Loyalist band of light horse infantry at dawn in Westchester County, New York, in May 1781. See the author's *From Slaves to Soldiers* (2016).

20. Although his father had temporarily lost the estate in a debt dispute as the war loomed, it was in the hands of Benjamin Gardiner during the war but later purchased back by the family.

21. List of Kentish Guards.

22. Richard Greene of Potowomut had twelve children, but Jonathan was not one of them. Thus the distinction "of Richard" rather than "son of…." Further, Greene was suspected of Tory sympathies, so much so that in 1776 the legislature sent an agent to his farm with empowerment of "purchasing of Mr. Richard Greene, the corn, oats, rye, pork and sheep he has on hand for the use of the state, and to remove the same to places of safety, and that if the said Richard Greene refuses to dispose of said articles to this state, the said James Arnold be empowered to take the same, allowing him therefore at the price fixed by this Assembly." RI Rec. 1776–79. Greene led a lavish lifestyle and had many servants, but his actions during the war threatened the seizure of his estate.

23. Rhode Island Historical Society Collections, vol. 5, F76, R47, Providence, Knowles and Vose, 1843, 248–49.

24. Chapman diary.

25. Providence Town Papers, "Return of Persons Able to Bear Arms in Providence."

26. Warwick Early Records, vol. 3, 148.

27. Both brothers would survive the war. Nathan married Nancy Warner in 1784, while Samuel married Candace Winsor in June 1778. Samuel and Candace appear on the 1790 census in Smithfield. They would have thirteen children and at some point moved the family to Herkimer, Monroe, New York, where Samuel died in 1831. Nathan's wife, Nancy, died on July 24, 1805, in Cumberland at the age of forty-two. They had one daughter named Pheobe. The date or whereabouts of Nathan's death remain unknown.

28. Fisher, *Liberty and Freedom*, 32–35.

29. Sparks, *Writings of George Washington*, vol. 1, 229.

30. Ballagh, *Letters of Richard Henry Lee*, vol. 1, 259.

Chapter 2

31. Higginbotham, *War and Society in Revolutionary America*, 111.

32. Ibid.

33. Holton, *Forced Founders*, 167.

34. Allen, "Kentish Guards."

35. Grandchamp, *Rhode Island Militia Battle*.

36. See Geake, *Cocumscussoc Reader*, 44–45.

37. White, *Connecticut's Black Soldiers*, 17, 18.

38. Cox, *Boy Soldiers in the American Revolution* 6.

39. MacGunnigle, "Thomas Mitchell."

40. Aubrecht, "History of the Drummer Boy."

41. While earlier historians believed the young man had died from his illness, records show John Anthony Aborn as a private in a company on duty at Pawtuxet in July 1778. One year later, he had been promoted to captain and betrothed to Sally Rhodes of another prominent Pawtuxet family.

42. Letter from Nathanael Greene to General Charles Lee, September 5, 1775, as cited in D'Amato's *Warwick* (2001). See also *Boston 1775* blog, "The Brief Army Career of John Anthony Aborn," November 11, 2016,

http://boston1775.blogspot.com/2016/11/the-brief-army-career-of-john-anthony.html.

43. Hafner, *Fife & Drums of the Lincoln Minute Men.*

44. Von Steuben, *Revolutionary War Drill Manual*, 89, 90.

45. Shattuck, "Prudence Wright and the Women." See also Fisher, *Paul Revere's Ride* (2005).

46. The men in the artillery units also needed water at a prodigious rate to wet the sponges on the rods that clean the cannon of gunpowder after firing. She was performing this duty at the Battle of Monmouth in June 1778. It was a sweltering day, and when her husband collapsed on the field from exhaustion, Mary picked up his ramrod while he was carried off the field and swabbed and loaded the cannon in his place as the battle continued. Joseph Plumb Martin would record her actions that day for posterity when he included the anecdote in his journal: "A woman whose husband belonged to the Artillery and who was then attached to a piece in the engagement, attended at the piece with her husband the whole time. While in the act of reaching a cartridge and having one of her feet as far before the other as she could step, a cannon shot from the enemy passed directly between her legs without doing any other damage but carrying away the lower part of her petticoat." Washington was so impressed by her courage that he later issued her a warrant as a noncommissioned officer, giving her the moniker of "Sergeant Molly" for the remainder of her life.

47. Ballagh, *Letters of Richard Henry Lee*, vol. 1, 203.

Chapter 3

48. Ibid., 209.

49. Buel, *Dear Liberty*, 31.

50. Cowell, *Spirit of '76 in Rhode Island*, 62, 63.

51. Buel, *Dear Liberty*, 112–14.

52. Ibid., 114.

53. Ibid., 115.

54. Buel and Buel, *Way of Duty*, 139.

55. Leete was the son of Pelatiah Leete (1681–1768) and grandson of Governor William Leete, who purchased but never settled on the island. Simeon's father moved the family there shortly after his marriage in 1705 and lived on the island for the remainder of his life. A year after losing his

father, Simeon lost three brothers as an epidemic swept through the town of Guilford, killing forty-four of its citizens.

56. Connecticut History, "Benedict Arnold Turns and Burns New London," connecticuthistory.org.

57. Thomas Verenna, "Explaining the Pennsylvania's Militia," *Journal of the American Revolution* (June 2014): 4.

58. Ibid., 7.

59. Ibid.

60. Ibid.

61. Showman, *Papers of Nathanael Greene*, vol. 2, 208.

62. As printed in Higginbotham, *War of American Independence*, 107.

63. Ballagh, *Letters of Richard Henry Lee*, vol. 1, 215.

64. Ibid., 286.

65. Nash, *Unknown American Revolution*, 218.

66. Ibid., 219.

67. Carolyn Lavallee, "Northbridge in the Revolutionary War Period," Northbridge Historical Society, August 2014, http://www.northbridgehistoricalsociety.com/rev-war-period.html.

68. The Vermont Constitution was written in the tavern a decade before the United States document that extended the right to vote to non-property owners and also outlawed slavery.

69. Smith, *Memoirs of Samuel Smith*, 7–8.

70. Ibid., 9.

71. Ibid.

72. Letter to General William Smallwood, March 16, 1778, in Showman, *Papers of Nathanael Greene*, vol. 2, 316.

73. Showman, *Papers of Nathanael Greene*, vol. 2, 359.

74. Ibid., 383.

75. Higginbotham, *War of American Independence*, 392.

76. Geake, *Fired a Gun at the Rising of the Sun*.

77. Beck, *War Before Independence*, 263–64.

78. Trumbull to Washington, December 7, 1775, in Twohig, *Papers of George Washington*, vol. 7.

79. McBurney, *Rhode Island Campaign*, 142.

80. Smith, *Memoirs of Samuel Smith*, 16–19.

81. Buel, *Dear Liberty*, 231–32.

82. Now South Salem, the area below the length of Truesdale Lake, close by the border with Connecticut.

83. Billias, *General John Glover*, 180.

84. Ibid., 181.
85. Thatcher, *Military Journal During the American Revolutionary War*, 240.
86. Ibid., 242.
87. Ibid.
88. Ibid., 243.
89. Ibid., 245–46.
90. Ibid.
91. LaCrosse, *Revolutionary Rangers*, 91–93.

Chapter 4

92. Fisher, *Washington's Crossing*, 25.
93. Ibid., 30.
94. Ibid.
95. *Maryland State Archives* blog, "Crime and Punishment in the Continental Army," "Finding the Maryland 400," July 28, 2017.
96. See Shepherd, "George Washington Convenes a Firing Squad."
97. Showman, *Papers of Nathanael Greene*, vol. 2, 74.
98. Ibid.
99. Thatcher, *Military Journal During the American Revolutionary War*, 145.
100. Procknow, "General Israel Putnam."
101. Ford, *General Orders Issued by Major-General Israel Putnam*, 5–6.
102. Ibid., 23.
103. Ibid., 38.
104. Prince, "Gallows Hill."
105. Rae, *People's War*, 216.
106. Ibid.
107. Ibid., 486–88.

Chapter 5

108. LaCrosse, *Revolutionary Rangers*, 5.
109. J.T. Headley, as quoted in Barnett, *Sacred Relics*, 29.
110. Ibid., 81–90.
111. Senter diary.
112. Ibid.
113. Topham diary.

114. Anthony Walker put the Rhode Island volunteers for Quebec at "about a hundred." The state also contributed Major Christopher Greene, promoted to lieutenant colonel, and Captains Simeon Thayer, John Topham and Samuel Ward, who together would command three of Arnold's musket companies. Most of the Rhode Islanders who volunteered were taken prisoner, including Lieutenant Colonel Greene and the three junior officers. Walker, *So Few the Brave*, 8–12.

115. Ibid.

116. Ballagh, *Letters of Richard Henry Lee*, vol. 1, 175.

117. Ibid., 130.

118. Rogers, Seidule and Watson, *West Point History of the American Revolution*, 81–83.

119. Rae, *People's War*, 229.

120. Ibid., 230.

121. Ewald and Tustin, *Diary of the American War*, 110.

122. Ibid.

123. LaCrosse, *Revolutionary Rangers*, 10.

124. Moore, *Diary of the American Revolution*.

125. Thatcher, *Military Journal During the American Revolutionary War*, 102–3.

126. LaCrosse, *Revolutionary Rangers*, 18.

127. Ibid., 21.

128. Twohig, *Papers of George Washington*, vol. 12, 284.

129. LaCrosse, *Revolutionary Rangers*, 20.

130. Letter from William Butler to George Clinton, August 13, 1778, *Public Papers of George Clinton*, vol. 3, 632.

131. Clark, *Onadaga*, 330–31. See also LaCrosse, *Revolutionary Rangers*, 40–43.

132. LaCrosse Jr. stated that these towns were on the southern shore of Onondaga Lake.

133. *The Order Book of Capt. Leonard Bleeker*, New York, 1865, 128

134. Rae, *People's War*, 383.

Chapter 6

135. Gardner, *Glover's Marblehead Regiment*, 1.

136. Fisher, *Washington's Crossing*, 21.

137. Gardner, *Glover's Marblehead Regiment*, 2.

138. Ibid., 2–3. Gardner cited Lossing as his source. A coat worn by Glover may be seen at the Museum in Eastchester, Pelham, New York.

139. Ibid., 4.

140. Billias, *General John Glover*, 89.

141. Ibid., 100–101.

142. Benjamin Lossing, Sandborn and F.A. Gardner all credit Glover's regiment with a successful evacuation in their early histories, with Gardner writing, "Between 9 o'clock on the night of the 13th, and sunrise on the next day, all the sick, numbering 500 were transferred to the Jersey shore." Gardner likewise has the brigade ferrying the baggage the following evening until Glover was called that night for Manhattan. George Billias, in his well-researched account, maintains that from the eyewitness account of Dr. John Morgan, the director general of the military hospital who actually helped offload wounded from the island, it was "[n]ot until the British invasion of Manhattan was actively underway were these casualties removed from the island. Glover's men were engaged in the fighting that day, and they could hardly have had time to evacuate any of the wounded."

143. As reprinted in Billias, *General John Glover*, 108.

144. Anderson, *Martyr and the Traitor*, 140.

145. Ibid., 148.

146. Billias, *General John Glover*, 111–12.

147. Ibid., 125.

148. John M. Shinn, "The Battle of Pell's Point, October 18, 1776," Pelham Historical Society, http://historicpelham.blogspot.com.

149. Billias, *General John Glover*, 126.

150. Upham, *Memoir of General John Glover*, 21.

151. Billias, *General John Glover*, 131.

152. Ibid., 133.

153. Letter to Jas. Warren, dated August 6, 1777, in Upham, *Memoir of General John Glover*, 26. See also Gardner, *Glover's Marblehead Regiment*, 11.

154. Ibid., 27.

155. Billias, *General John Glover*, 141.

156. Ibid., 143.

157. Ibid., 153.

158. Ibid., 166.

159. Ibid., 172.

160. Ibid., 173.

Chapter 7

161. Polhemus and Polhemus, *Stark*, 159.
162. Ibid., 164.
163. Ibid., 167.
164. Ibid., 169.
165. Ibid., 188.
166. Stanley, *Canada Invaded, 1775–1776*, 128.
167. Beebe, *Journal of Dr. Lewis Beebe*, 333.
168. Polhemus and Polhemus, *Stark*, 195.
169. Beebe, *Journal of Dr. Lewis Beebe*, 325–26.
170. Ibid., 340.
171. Letter of George Washington to the Continental Congress, July 16, 1776, *American Archives*, 5th series, vol. 1, 234.
172. Polhemus and Polhemus, *Stark*, 201.
173. Ibid., 205–6.
174. Beebe, *Journal of Dr. Lewis Beebe*, 357.
175. Polhemus and Polhemus, *Stark*, 218.
176. Ibid., 219. See also Dwyer, *The Day Is Ours!*, 139–40.
177. Polhemus and Polhemus, *Stark*, 230.
178. Ibid., 242.
179. Stark, *Memoir and Correspondence*, 127–28.
180. Polhemus and Polhemus, *Stark*, 252.

Chapter 8

181. Howe, *Col. John Brown, of Pittsfield, Massachusetts*, 1908.
182. A local story has it that the elderly Johnson, on the eve of the Revolution he knew was coming, was compelled to rise from his sickbed on July 11, 1774, to address some six hundred Iroquois who had gathered at his estate, Johnson Hall. He urged them, "Whatever may happen, you must not be shaken out of your shoes," and according to local historians, after ordering pipes, tobacco and liquor for the warriors, he retired to his chamber, where he "gulped some water and wine, slumped into a chair, and with his head back, sighed his last breath." See Foote and Storm, *Gateway to Freedom*.
183. Peter Force, *American Archives*, 4th Series, vol. 2, 244.

184. Fort Ticonderoga, "Mounted Soldiers in Brown's Raid," September 12, 2013, https://www.forticonderoga.org/blog/mounted-soldiers-in-browns-raid.

185. Ibid.

186. Howe's address stated that the barracks held 200 men, but as Brown was in command of approximately 380 men, we can assume that there was a large encampment within, and likely outside of, the fort as well.

187. Report of Sir John Johnston, October 31, 1780, Montreal, as reprinted in Cruikshank and Watt, *History and Muster Roll of the Kings Regiment*, 51–55.

188. Garret L. Roof, *Colonel John Brown, His Service in the Revolutionary War, Battle of Stone Arabia*, An Address Delivered before the Oneida Historical Society, April 28, 1884.

189. Berry, *Fort Plain & Fort Plank*, 50.

190. Foote and Storm, *Gateway to Freedom*, 91.

191. Watt, *Burning of the Valleys*, 306.

192. Ibid., 207.

193. Ibid.

194. Foote and Storm, *Gateway to Freedom*, 94.

195. Ibid.

Epilogue

196. Higginbotham, *War of American Independence*, 116.

197. Ibid., 114.

198. Coffman, *Old Army*, 3.

199. Weld, *Travels through the States of North America*, vol. 2, 95, 97.

200. *Trials by Court Martial of Capt. Samuel Watson*, 30.

201. Ibid., 66–67.

202. Ibid., 67.

203. Wikipedia, "Rhode Island National Guard," https://en.wikipedia.org/wiki/Rhode_Island_National_Guard.

BIBLIOGRAPHY

Allen, Colonel Thomas. "Kentish Guards: A History." In *Four Documents on the History of the Kentish Guards*. Edited by Richard Sheryka. Warwick, RI: privately printed, 2015.

Anderson, Virginia DeJohn. *The Martyr and the Traitor: Nathan Hale, Moses Dunbar, and the American Revolution*. New York: Oxford University Press, 2017.

Ballagh, James Curtis, ed. *The Letters of Richard Henry Lee*. 2 vols. New York: Da Capo Press, 1970.

Barnett, Teresa. *Sacred Relics: Pieces of the Past in Nineteenth-Century America*. Chicago: University of Chicago Press, 2013.

Beck, Derek W. *The War Before Independence, 1775–1776*. N.p.: Sourcebooks, 2016.

Beebe, Lewis. *Journal of Dr. Lewis Beebe: Eyewitness Accounts of the American Revolution*. New York: New York Times, 1974.

Bell, J.L. *The Road to Concord: How Four Stolen Cannons Ignited the Revolutionary War*. Yardley, PA: Westholme Publishing, 2016.

Berry, A.J. *Fort Plain & Fort Plank: Two Fort Plain Revolutionary War Forts in the Words of Those Who Served New York*. New York: Fort Plain Museum, 2013.

Billias, George Athan. *General John Glover and His Marblehead Mariners*. New York: Holt, Rinehart, and Winston, 1960.

Buel, Richard, Jr. *Dear Liberty: Connecticut's Mobilization for the Revolutionary War*. Middletown, CT: Wesleyan University Press, 1980.

Buel, Richard, Jr., and Joy Buel. *The Way of Duty: A Woman and Her Family in Revolutionary America.* New York: Norton & Company, 1980.

Clark, Joshua V.H. *Onadaga, or, Reminiscences of Earlier and Later Times.* Syracuse, NY, 1849.

Coffman, Edward M. *The Old Army: A Portrait of the American Army in Peacetime, 1784–1898.* New York: Oxford University Press, 1986.

Cowell, Benjamin. *Spirit of '76 in Rhode Island, or, Sketches of the Efforts of the Government and People in the War of Revolution.* Boston: A.J. Wright, 1850.

Cox, Caroline. *Boy Soldiers in the American Revolution.* Chapel Hill: University of North Carolina Press, 2016.

Cruikshank, Brigadier General Ernet A., and Gavin K. Watt. *The History and Muster Roll of the Kings Regiment of New York.* N.p.: Global Heritage Press, 2006.

D'Amato, Donald A. *Warwick: A City at the Crossroads.* Charleston, SC: Arcadia Publishing, 2001.

Dwyer, William M. *The Day Is Ours!: An Inside View of the Battles of Trenton and Princeton, November 1776–January 1777.* New Brunswick, NJ: Rutgers University Press, 1998.

Ewald, Johann, with Joseph P. Tustin, ed. *Diary of the American War: A Hessian Journal.* New Haven, CT: Yale University Press, 1979.

Field, Edward. *Revolutionary Defenses in Rhode Island.* Providence, RI: Preston & Rounds, 1896.

Fisher, David Hackett. *Liberty and Freedom: A Visual History of America's Founding Ideas.* New York: Oxford University Press, 2005.

———. *Paul Revere's Ride.* New York: Oxford University Press, 2005.

———. *Washington's Crossing.* New York: Oxford University Press, 2004.

Foote, Alland D., and Geoffrey Storm. *Gateway to Freedom: The American Revolution on the Northern Frontier.* N.p.: Mohawk Valley History Project, Northern Frontier Project, 2005.

Ford, Worthington Chauncey, ed. *General Orders Issued by Major-General Israel Putnam, When in Command of the Highlands, in the Summer and Fall of 1777.* Boston: Gregg Press, 1972.

Gardner, F.A. *Glover's Marblehead Regiment in the War of the Revolution.* Salem, MA: Salem Press, 1908.

Geake, Robert A. *A Cocumscussoc Reader.* Providence, RI: Footprints Press, 2017.

———. *Fired a Gun at the Rising of the Sun: The Diary of Noah Robinson of Attleborough in the Revolutionary War.* Providence, RI: Footprints Press, 2018.

Goodrich, John E., ed. *Rolls of the Soldiers in the Revolutionary War, 1775–1783*. Rutland, VT: Tuttle Company, 1904.

Higginbotham, Don. *War and Society in Revolutionary America: The Wider Dimensions of Conflict*. Chapel Hill: University of North Carolina Press, 1988.

———. *The War of American Independence: Military Attitudes, Policies and Practices*. New York: MacMillan, 1971.

Holton, Woody. *Forced Founders: Indians, Debtors, Slaves, & the Making of the American Revolution in Virginia*. Chapel Hill: University of North Carolina Press, 1999.

Howe, Archibald Murray. *Col. John Brown of Pittsfield Massachusetts, the Brave Accuser of Benedict Arnold: An Address Delivered before the Fort Rensselaer Chapter of the D.A.R. and Others…*. Boston: W.B. Clark Company, 1908.

Humphrey, William. "A Journal in the Year 1775–1776." In *Rhode Islanders Record the Revolution: The Journals of William Humphrey and Zuriel Waterman*. Providence: Rhode Island Publication Society, 1984.

LaCrosse, Richard B. *Revolutionary Rangers: Daniel Morgan's Riflemen and Their Role on the Northern Frontier*. Westminster, CT: Heritage Books, 2007.

McBurney, Christian. *The Rhode Island Campaign*. Yardley, PA: Westholme Publishing, 2011.

Moore, Frank, ed. *Diary of the American Revolution from Newspapers and Original Documents*. New York: Charles Scribner, 1860.

Nash, Gary. *The Unknown American Revolution: The Unruly Birth of Democracy and the Struggle to Create America*. New York: Viking Press, 2005.

Polhemus, Richard, and John Polhemus. *Stark: The Life and Wars of John Stark, French and Indian War Ranger, Revolutionary War General*. New York: Black Dome Press, 2014.

Rae, Noel. *The People's War: Original Voices of the American Revolution*. Guilford, CT: Lyman's Press, 2012.

Raphael, Ray. "Country Crowds in Revolutionary Massachusetts: Mobs and Militia." *Journal of the American Revolution* (Annual Volume 2018).

Rogers, Seidule, Watson, ed. *The West Point History of the American Revolution*. New York: Simon & Schuster, 2016.

Roof, Garret L. "Colonel John Brown, His Service in the Revolutionary War, Battle of Stone Arabia." An Address Delivered before the Oneida Historical Society, April 28, 1884.

Shattuck, Mary Lucinda Parker. "Prudence Wright and the Women Who Guarded the Bridge." In *The Story of Jewett's Bridge*. N.p.: privately printed, 1912.

Sheryka, Colonel Richard. *Four Documents on the History of the Kentish Guard.* East Greenwich, RI: Varnum Museum, 2015.

Showman, Richard K., ed. *The Papers of Nathanael Greene.* Vol. 2. Chapel Hill: University of North Carolina Press, for the Rhode Island Historical Society, 1980.

Smith, Joseph Jenckes. *Civil and Military List of Rhode Island, 1647–1800.* 2 vols. Providence, RI: Preston & Rounds, 1900.

Smith, Samuel. *Memoirs of Samuel Smith, a Soldier of the Revolution, 1776–1786.* New York: privately printed, 1860.

Sparks, Stuart, ed. *The Writings of George Washington: Being His Correspondence, Addresses, Messages, and Other Papers, Official and Private.* Reprint, Arcos Press, 2015.

Stanley, George. *Canada Invaded, 1775–1776.* Toronto: Hackert Press, 1973.

Stark, Caleb, ed. *Memoir and Correspondence of General John Stark.* Concord, MA: G. Parker Lyon, 1860.

Thatcher, James. *A Military Journal during the Revolutionary War, from 1775–1783.* Plymouth, MA: privately printed, 1827.

Upham, William P. *A Memoir of General John Glover, of Marblehead.* Salem, MA: Charles W. Swasey, 1863.

Von Steuben, Frederick William Baron. *Revolutionary War Drill Manual.* New York: Dover, 1985.

Walker, Anthony. *So Few the Brave: Rhode Island Continentals, 1775–1783.* Newport: Rhode Island Society of the Sons of the American Revolution, 1981.

Watt, Gavin K. *The Burning of the Valleys: Daring Raids from Canada Against the New York Frontier in the Fall of 1780.* Toronto: Dundurn Press, 1997.

Weld, Isaac. *Travels through the States of North America and the Provinces of Upper and Lower Canada during the years 1795, 1796, and 1797.* London: John Stockdale, 1897.

White, David O. *Connecticut's Black Soldiers, 1775–1783.* Guilford, CT: Pequot Press, 1973.

Primary Source Documents

Chapman, Zerviah (Sanger), Diary, 1775–83. Rhode Island Historical Society, Misc. Collections, 9001-C.

List of Kentish Guards, January 1, 1775. Rhode Island Historical Society, MSS 675 Series 5, Box 3, F 105.

Providence Town Papers. Series 2, vol. 3. Item 0885, "Return of Persons Able to Bear Arms in Providence," February 10, 1776.

Senter, Dr. Isaac, Diary. Rhode Island Historical Society Manuscript Collection, MSS 165 S5 B2 F6.

State of New York. *Public Papers of George Clinton, First Governor of New York, 1777–1795—1801–1804*. Vol. 3. Albany, NY, 1909.

Sylvanus, Martin Diary. Rhode Island Historical Society Manuscript Collection, MSS 9001-S.

Topham, Colonel John, Diary. Rhode Island Historical Society Manuscript Collection, MSS 9001-T.

Trials by Court Martial of Capt. Samuel Watson 2d, David Livermore, Daniel Kent, and William Prouty: of the 1st Reg. 1st Brig. and 7th Division of Massachusetts Militia, 1810. Worcester, MA: Henry Rogers, 1811.

Twohig, Dorothy, ed. *The Papers of George Washington. Presidential Series*. Vol. 7, *October 1776–January 1777*. Charlottesville: University Press of Virginia, 1987.

Warwick Early Records. Town Books, vol. 3. Warwick Historical Society.

Wright Captain Robert K., Jr. *Massachusetts Militia Roots: A Bibliographic Study*. Departments of the Army and the Air Force Historical Services Branch, 1986.

Periodicals

Aubrecht, Michael. "The History of the Drummer Boy." *Modern Drummer Magazine* (n.d.).

MacGunnigle, Bruce. "Thomas Mitchell, Fifer in the 2nd Rhode Island Regiment." *The Encampment Newsletter*, January 21, 1986.

Online Sources

Grandchamp, Robert. *Rhode Island Militia Battle the Dreaded British Captain James Wallace on Prudence Island*. Online Review of Rhode Island History, November 2, 2018. http://www.smallstatebighistory.com.

Hafner, Donald L. *The Fife & Drums of the Lincoln Minutemen through History*. http://www2bc.edu

Prince, Cathryn J. "Gallows Hill: The 1779 Executions of Edward Jones and John Smith." *Journal of the American Revolution* (September 2, 2013). http://www.allthingsliberty.com.

Procknow, Gene. "General Israel Putnam: Reputation Revisited." *Journal of the American Revolution* (August 11, 2016). http://www.allthingsliberty.com.

Robertson, John K. "Decoding Connecticut Militia, 1739–1783." *Journal of the American Revolution* (July 2016). http://www.allthingsliberty.com.

Shepherd, Joshua. "George Washington Convenes a Firing Squad." *Journal of the American Revolution* (February 9, 2016). http://allthingsliberty.com.

INDEX

The author, as photographed for the *Newport Daily News* during a ceremony at Patriot's Park in Portsmouth, Rhode Island, site of the monument to the First Rhode Island Regiment. *Photograph by Louis Walker III.*